"Mark Jones's book is highly importa[ ] Reformed is much more than just being Contra-Remonstrant. Thanks to his vast knowledge of historical theology, he ably shows the well-defined Reformed response against antinomianism, and the relevance of the theme for today."

—**Gert van den Brink**, author, *Herman Witsius en het Antinomianisme*

"We are living in a deeply encouraging day when the sovereignty of God's grace is being rediscovered far and wide. But as has happened in the past, when such times of biblical *ressourcement* have occurred, the error of anti-nomianism has made its appearance. This new work by Mark Jones is thus a timely tract for the times. It is rich in scriptural argument, illustrations from church history, and vigorous application. May it have a wide reading and even wider heeding!"

—**Michael A. G. Haykin**, Professor of Church History and Biblical Spirituality, The Southern Baptist Theological Seminary

"Church history records that the doctrinal pendulum often swings from one dangerous extreme to the other. This present day is no exception. The legalistic abuses of recent decades are now being replaced with a hyper-grace license to sin. Sad to say, portions of the Reformed community have given shelter to this new antinomianism, claiming that personal obedience to the law of Christ is merely optional. Often trendy with 'the young, restless, and Reformed,' this toxic message is poisonous to the soul. In this excellent work, Mark Jones exercises considerable skill in exposing the fatal flaws of this anti-law, cheap-grace easy-believism. Throughout these pages, you will find the theological clarity needed to reject the twisted errors of legalism and license and embrace a true, grace-inspired, Spirit-empowered obedience to the Scripture."

—**Steven J. Lawson**, Senior Pastor, Christ Fellowship Baptist Church, Mobile, Alabama

"Law-and-gospel issues continue to claim center stage in our time, as they have in the past. The much-cited adage 'he who can distinguish law and gospel is a theologian' has never been more appropriate than now, and on this count Mark Jones is a very fine theologian indeed. A carefully nuanced analysis of the Scylla of antinomianism and the Charybdis of legalism from a masterly guide. Essential reading."

> —**Derek Thomas**, Professor of Historical and Systematic Theology, Reformed Theological Seminary, Atlanta; Minister of Preaching and Teaching, First Presbyterian Church, Columbia, South Carolina

"The problem of antinomianism is a hardy perennial for the church. A mischievous movement is afoot at the moment—its soaring rhetoric about grace is matched by an equally casual presumption on grace. Mark Jones's book is thus to be welcomed: it is biblically grounded, historically sensitive, and above all timely. In addition, through his careful attention to the role of Christ in Scripture and to historical Reformed confessional treatments of sanctification, Jones provides a significant supplement to other recent books pleading for a biblical emphasis on personal piety."

> —**Carl R. Trueman**, Paul Woolley Professor of Church History, Westminster Theological Seminary

"Mark Jones's book offers a balanced treatment of the errors of antinomianism, not only as it surfaced among some seventeenth-century British and New England theologians, but also as it has resurfaced among some contemporary theologians. The strength of Jones's case lies in his nuanced definition of the error of antinomianism. Though in the popular imagination antinomianism is often simply identified with a denial of the positive role of God's moral law in the Christian life, Jones demonstrates that it includes a number of additional elements—a belittling of Christ's example of holiness as a pattern for the Christian life (*imitatio Christi*); a diminishment of the law of God as a true means of sanctification; an unbalanced conception of the relationship between law and gospel; a reluctance to acknowledge the biblical emphasis on rewards as a legitimate motive for Christian obedience; and a failure to recognize the role of good works as a secondary ground for the believer's assurance of salvation. But the principal strength of Jones's argument against antinomianism resides in his emphasis on the fullness of Christ's person and saving work. Jones shows how a proper understanding of the work of Christ includes the gospel benefits of free justification and progressive sanctification. In doing so, Jones nicely exposes one of the ironies of antinomianism—in the name of preserving the gospel, antinomianism typically truncates it."

—**Cornelis P. Venema**, President and Professor of Doctrinal Studies, Mid-America Reformed Seminary

"What does a seventeenth-century theological controversy have to do with Christian living in the twenty-first century? Everything. With the acumen of a historian and the heart of a pastor, Mark Jones deftly guides readers through one of the most tangled and important set of issues facing the Reformed church today. If you want to preach the gospel with greater biblical clarity, or learn how better to apply the gospel to your daily life, pick up this book and begin reading."

—**Guy Prentiss Waters**, Professor of New Testament, Reformed Theological Seminary, Jackson

ANTINOMIANISM

ANTINOMIANISM

REFORMED THEOLOGY'S
UNWELCOME GUEST?

MARK JONES

P U B L I S H I N G
P.O. BOX 817 • PHILLIPSBURG • NEW JERSEY 08865-0817

ISBN: 978-1-59638-815-4 (pbk.)
ISBN: 978-1-59638-816-1 (ePub)
ISBN: 978-1-59638-817-8 (Mobi)

Printed in the United States of America

Library of Congress Cataloging-in-Publication Data

Jones, Mark, 1980-
  Antinomianism : reformed theology's unwelcome guest? / Mark Jones. -- 1st ed.
    pages cm
  Includes bibliographical references and index.
  ISBN 978-1-59638-815-4 (pbk.)
  1. Antinomianism. I. Title.
  BT1330.J66 2013
  230'.42--dc23
                            2013024135

For:
Colin Taylor
Corrie Krahn
Don Robertson
Jed Schoepp
Jonathan Bos

CONTENTS

FOREWORD

CHRISTIANITY IS THE FAITH in Jesus Christ that mastered the hearts, minds, and lives of the New Testament writers. This faith portrays personal salvation from sin as coming to lost mankind through the mediatorial ministry of Jesus Christ the Lord, whereby a new humanity is being created and a full reconstruction of our sin-spoiled cosmos is guaranteed. By the fifth century, the world church was clear that the New Testament faith was Trinitarian, with Jesus being the second person of the eternal Three-in-One, and was also incarnational, with Jesus' redemptive role resting on his being fully God and fully man. For the next millennium, the church stood steady on these truths. The sixteenth-century Reformation introduced detailed, Bible-based corrections to what had become the conventional conceptualizing of them, and what was arguably the most accurate of these endeavors, namely the Reformed school of thought, began to generate the intense theological energy and the equally intense Christ-centered piety that marks it still.

However, just as the Reformed have seen a need to cross swords with Roman Catholics, Eastern Orthodox, Protestant Arminians, and (less violently) Lutherans and Baptists, so have they experienced their own internal dissensions. In this fallen world, where forces of both intellectual and moral corruption are constantly abroad, this was to be expected, and it has certainly occurred. The cluster of deviations that bears the name antinomianism is a case in point.

Antinomians among the Reformed have always seen themselves as reacting in the name of free grace against a hangover of legalistic, works-based bondage in personal discipleship. Characteristically, they have affirmed, not that the Mosaic law, under which Jesus lived and which was basic to his own moral teaching, does not after all state God's true standards for human living, but that it and its sanctions have no direct relevance to us once we have closed with Christ. Distinctive to Reformed theology from its birth has been its insistence that salvation, both relationally in justification and transformationally in sanctification, is ours entirely by virtue of our grace-given union with Christ in his death and resurrection—a union that God the Holy Spirit creates and sustains. Within this biblical framework, the key error of antinomianism in all its forms has been to treat our union with Christ as involving in effect some degree of personal absorption into Christ, such that the law as a voice from God no longer speaks to us or of us directly. From this starting point, the phalanx of antinomian teachers has spread out, celebrating different aspects of the assured confidence and joy in Christ that this supposedly biblical move of muzzling the law is thought to have opened up for us.

Thus, with regard to justification, antinomians affirm that God never sees sin in believers; once we are in Christ, whatever our subsequent lapses, he sees at every moment only the flawless righteousness of the Savior's life on earth, now reckoned as ours. Then, with regard to sanctification, there have been mystical antinomians who have affirmed that the indwelling Christ is the personal subject who obeys the law in our identity once we invoke his help in obedience situations, and there have been pneumatic antinomians who have affirmed that the Holy Spirit within us directly prompts us to discern and do the will of God, without our needing to look to the law to either prescribe or monitor our performance. The common ground is that those who live in Christ are wholly separated from every aspect of the pedagogy of the law. The freedom with which Christ has set us free, and the entire source of our ongoing peace and assurance, are based upon our knowledge that what Christ, as we say, enables us to do he actually does in us for himself. So now we live, not by being for-given our constant shortcomings, but by being out of the law's bailiwick altogether; not by imitating Christ, the archetypal practitioner of holy obedience to God's law, but by burrowing ever deeper into the joy of our free justification, and of our knowledge that Christ himself actually does in us all that his and our Father wants us to do. Thus the correlating of conscience with the Father's coded commands and Christ's own casuistry of compassion need not and indeed should not enter into the living of the Christian life, as antinomians understand it.

The bottom line of all this? The conclusion of the matter? Here, as elsewhere, the reaction of man does not lead to the righteousness of God, but rather obstructs holiness. In God's family, as in human families, an antinomian attitude to parental law makes for pride and immaturity, misbehavior and folly. Our true model of wise godliness, as well as our true mediator of God's grace, is Jesus Christ, our law-keeping Lord.

Mark Jones's monograph is the work of a Puritan-minded scholar and theologian who understands these things well, has researched historic antinomianism with thoroughness, and has many illuminating things to say about it. His book is a pioneering overview that I commend most warmly, particularly to pastors. Why to them? Start reading it, and you will soon see.

J. I. Packer

PREFACE

IN A BOOK ON ANTINOMIANISM, every sentence counts, because this is a topic that, by its very nature, has produced as much heat as it has light since the time of the Reformation. Nonetheless, books on antinomianism are few and far between. Apart from strictly academic works, not many books have been written in the twentieth and twenty-first centuries specifically devoted to the subject.[1] The academic works which attempt to analyze antinomianism are typically descriptive in nature, though there are certain social historians who cannot help but comment on the truths or errors of certain groups.

This book aims to move us beyond the notion that antinomians deny that God's moral law is binding on Christians in the new covenant. While they may deny that the threefold use of the law is biblical, or that the law of Moses has been replaced with the law of Christ, few theologians, pastors, or Christian laypersons would deny the plain teaching of Ephesians 6:1–3, where children are told to obey their parents in the Lord. There are literally hundreds of imperatives in the New Testament. For that reason, the idea that people are against God's law (hence, "antinomian"), however that is conceived, may seem like much ado about nothing in Bible-believing circles, particularly in Reformed and Presbyterian churches.

The following chapters will demonstrate, however, that antinomianism is a system of thought that has to be carefully understood in its historical context, rather than simply according to its etymology. Thus, the first chapter shows what antinomianism looks like historically. Those

---

1. Perhaps Andrew Fuller's sentiment explains why this is so: "There is something so low, foul, and scurrilous in the generality of the advocates of this system [i.e., Antinomianism], that few have cared to encounter them, lest they should bring upon themselves a torrent of abuse." Andrew Fuller, *Antinomianism Contrasted With the Religion Taught and Exemplified in the Holy Scriptures in The Works of Andrew Fuller* (Edinburgh: Banner of Truth Trust, 2007), 335.

with some expertise in post-Reformation Reformed theology are likely to pick up on the subtleties of antinomian thinking that is abroad today. For that reason, several chapters are given to specifically antinomian concerns.

In Puritan England, antinomianism threatened to undermine the foundations of moral and social order (i.e., the normative creational perspective). That would need to be discussed in a purely historical study of antinomianism. But because of the Christological focus of this book, the law as an abiding rule for society in general will not be specifically treated. Nonetheless, in order to evaluate several key theological tenets of antinomianism, we will examine its growth in Britain and New England during the seventeenth century. By that time, many precious truths that had been discovered and rediscovered in the Reformation and post-Reformation eras were being taken in directions that were decidedly un-Reformed and unbiblical. The various threats of Roman Catholicism, Arminianism, and Socinianism were very much alive in England around the time of the Westminster Assembly (1640s), but the Westminster divines found themselves having to contend with an equally pernicious theology that they termed "antinomianism." The writings of the divines, as well as other Reformed theologians in Britain and on the Continent, reveal that antinomianism was not simply a rejection of the moral law, but a wholesale departure from Reformed orthodoxy on several points of doctrine.

In assessing antinomianism, therefore, the right questions need to be asked in order to get the right answers. Simply affirming that there are passages in the Bible that speak about God's role in salvation and human responsibility in the Christian life will not suffice. The problem of antinomianism is an acute one, and its errors need to be exposed by making sure that specific questions are asked. The following chapters attempt to do just that. It should be added that this book is not strictly historical theology. It is not merely an attempt to recount the facts of history, a labor that has been accomplished ably in several academic works to date, but also an attempt to evaluate that history (i.e., prescriptively), and so it falls within the realm of systematic theology.

Antinomianism was the lifelong bogeyman of Richard Baxter (1615–91). He believed that he was called by God to deliver the Reformed world, not only from the practical antinomianism (i.e., "loose living") that he witnessed in different contexts, but also from the theological antinomianism that was finding its way into pulpits and books. While I have great admiration and respect for Baxter's ministry, his case is somewhat ironic. His view of justification slipped in a "neonomian" direction.[2] It is useless to combat one error with another; the example of Baxter shows that critiquing a system of theology exposes the polemicist to the real temptation of going too far in the opposite direction.

The grace of God in salvation must be maintained at all costs. On that we are all agreed, I hope. Indeed, even Roman Catholics and Arminians would agree with that sentiment. Specifically, then, the "aloneness" of faith as the instrument by which we receive the righteousness of Christ imputed to us must be upheld, even if it costs us our reputations or lives. Spirit-wrought, imparted righteousness is not enough for us; we also need a perfect righteousness that is better than our own. But, at the same time, the robust doctrine of sanctification that has characterized Reformed orthodoxy for centuries, and which has been and continues to be attacked even in broadly Reformed circles, must likewise be defended. This is not a book on holiness or sanctification per se, but by analyzing and critiquing antinomianism, this work will provide readers with a theological framework within which to approach the Scriptures and make sense of passages that sometimes are explained away in the most ingenious ways. There are a number of topics related to this discussion that are not included in this book. I have chosen to be selective, not exhaustive.

As someone with some scholarly acquaintance with post-Reformation Reformed theology, particularly in the area of Puritanism, I have been dismayed at some of the theology that passes as Reformed, when in fact it has corollaries to seventeenth-century antinomianism. I have chosen not to name names, but there are a few exceptions to this principle in the book. Rather, my aim is to help readers, particularly pastors, understand certain tenets of antinomianism, which will allow them to connect the dots, so

---

2. Like antinomianism, neonomianism is a complex theological phenomenon. In short, it is the idea that Christ, by fulfilling the requirements of the old covenant, makes it possible for man to be justified according to the more lenient terms of the "new law" (hence, "neonomianism") of the gospel. Christ's righteous obedience becomes the meritorious cause of justification, which allows the faith of the believer to be the formal cause of justification. By contrast, most Reformed theologians believed that the imputation of Christ's righteousness was the formal cause of justification. See Richard Baxter, *A Treatise of Justifying Righteousness in Two Books* (London: Nevil Simons & Jonathan Robinson, 1676); Hans Boersma, *A Hot Pepper Corn: Richard Baxter's Doctrine of Justification in Its Seventeenth-Century Context of Controversy* (Vancouver: Regent College Publishing, 2003).

to speak, in the contemporary scene. I make no apologies for depending upon Reformed authors. We will see how various Reformed luminaries from different countries in different eras have addressed such topics as the law, the gospel, and good works. Yet there is always room for advancement and clarification in our tradition. In a few areas, especially in relation to Christological concerns, I try to make explicit what has been implicit in a number of Reformed writers over the years. Nonetheless, my commitment to the Westminster Standards is resolute, and so this work unashamedly fits in the Westminster (Puritan) tradition.

As a pastor, I have also seen the benefit of preaching the whole Christ. In fact, the more I have had a chance to understand the person and work of Christ, the more I have been free to preach sermons that do justice not only to Christ's office as priest, but also to his offices as prophet and king. Good Christology and good application are not enemies, but friends. Bad Christology leads to bad or no application. As readers will (I hope) see, a Reformed understanding of Christ's person and work—not necessarily more imperatives, though they belong in our preaching—is the true solution to the problem of antinomianism. This issue is above all a pastoral one, and there would be no reason to write a book on such a controversial subject if people's souls were not at risk. But love for Christ demands that his glory and honor be defended. For that reason, and that reason alone, I have been drawn into this controversy.

Finally, my own attitude toward those whom I consider to be antinomians or to have leanings in that direction is best summed up by the following from Samuel Rutherford (1600–1661):

> If Antinomians offend, or such as are, out of ignorance, seduced, hate me for heightening Christ, not in a Gospel-licence, as they do; but in a strict and accurate walking, in commanding of which, both law and gospel do friendly agree, and never did, and never could jar, or contest; I threaten them, in this I write, with the revenge of good will, to have them saved, in a weak aim, and a far off, at least, desire, to offer to their view such a Gospel-Idea, and representation of Christ, as the Prophets and Apostles have shown in the word of his Kingdom, who opens the secrets of the Father to the sons of men.[3]

---

3. Samuel Rutherford, *Christ dying and drawing sinners to himself* (London, 1647), "To the Reader."

ACKNOWLEDGMENTS

THE EFFORT that went into writing this book was not mine alone. I was helped and encouraged by Bob McKelvey, Mark Herzer, Gert van den Brink, Ruben Zartman, Matthew Winzer, Ian Clary, Ted van Raalte, Paul Walker, Benji Swinburnson, D. Patrick Ramsey, and Ryan McGraw. In different ways they contributed to what merit there may be in this work.

I offer a special thank you to Professor David Garner of Westminster Theological Seminary. He first contacted me about writing a book for P&R Publishing. Eventually I decided on this topic, but without David's help this book may not have been realized. Also many thanks to Jared Oliphint for his encouragement as he read portions of this book before it came to print. Thank you also to Paul Mandry for the inspiration to finish this book.

I would also like to recognize my congregation at Faith Vancouver Presbyterian Church (PCA) for their desire to hear Christ preached. My great privilege as a minister of the gospel is to preach the unsearchable riches of Christ Jesus. Their great privilege is to know and love Christ. We have, I hope, all come to love Christ's person and his work more and more over the years.

P&R Publishing has been a delight to work with. Amanda Martin and John Hughes have ensured that things run smoothly during the difficult process of bringing a book to press. There are others behind the scenes at P&R who also deserve my gratitude. They know who they are, and I am deeply grateful for how diligently they all worked with me on this book.

Thanking my family is always a joy. My four children (Katie, Josh, Thomas, and Matthew) bring delight to me in ways I cannot express in words. And my wife, Barbara, is nothing short of heroic as a wife and mother. I simply ask their forgiveness for the antinomian tendencies that remain in my own heart.

Finally, I wish to praise the one who is "chief among ten thousand," who is God over all, for enabling me to write of his person and work in a manner that, I pray, will bring glory to his name—the name that is above every name.

EDITOR'S NOTES

NOTE THAT OLD ENGLISH spelling and grammar have generally been modernized. All quotations from the Bible come from the English Standard Version (ESV), unless a quote comes from an author in a previous century.

The abbreviation WCF is used for the Westminster Confession of Faith, and WLC is used for the Westminster Larger Catechism.

1

LESSONS FROM HISTORY

"PLUS ÇA CHANGE, PLUS C'EST LA MÊME CHOSE."

THE FIRST ANTINOMIANS

Adam was the first antinomian (Rom. 5). In the garden, he was against (*anti*) God's law (*nomos*) when he transgressed by failing to guard the garden and to forbid his wife to eat from the tree of the knowledge of good and evil. Eve's own doctrinal antinomianism (Gen. 3:2–3) led to practical antinomianism (3:6). Thus, antinomianism was birthed by our original parents. Interestingly, though, their antinomianism was in response to Satan's legalism, for it was he who had (willfully) misconstrued God's gracious loving-kindness to Adam and Eve and made God out to be a legalist, reflecting his own heart (3:1–5).

The Scottish theologian John "Rabbi" Duncan (1796–1870) has rightly argued that "there is only one heresy, and that is Antinomianism," for all sin, including heresy, is against God's law.[1] The apostle John essentially makes this point when he says that sin is lawlessness (*anomia*) (1 John 3:4). A history of antinomianism, when defined this way, could easily be derived from the Bible. Similarly, antinomianism, viewed either as breaking or opposing God's law, is the picture of society at large and regrettably even the church. Nonetheless, the theological concept of antinomianism is a

---

1. John Duncan, *Colloquia Peripatetica* (Edinburgh: Edmonston & Douglas, 1873), 70.

lot more complex than simply being against God's law, either doctrinally or practically.[2]

Most people assume that the Pharisees were the preeminent legalists—that is, those who are generally considered to be the opposite of antinomians—trusting in their own obedience more than God's grace. Some modern scholars, however, have tried to play down the legalistic elements in Second Temple Judaism. In their view, Paul was not concerned so much with self-righteousness as with Jewish nationalism in the form of certain boundary markers (e.g., circumcision, dietary laws, and the Sabbath). While there is some truth in these reassessments, the fundamental problem was still self-righteousness and legalism. Those boundary markers were symptoms of a larger problem: a legalistic heart. But the problem was at the same time antinomianism. Christ makes this clear in Matthew 23:23, "Woe to you, scribes and Pharisees, hypocrites! For you tithe mint and dill and cumin, and have neglected the weightier matters of the law: justice and mercy and faithfulness. These you ought to have done, without neglecting the others." The Pharisees did not actually keep the law (Mark 7:8); their Talmudic legalism actually made them practical antinomians insofar as they "neglected the weightier matters of the law: justice and mercy and faithfulness." They loved the praise of men more than the praise of God (John 12:43); they were self-seeking, dishonest, murderous hypocrites (Matt. 23). Far from keeping the law, they were lawbreakers, and this culminated in what would be the greatest crime in history, the killing of the only completely innocent man ever to live—Jesus of Nazareth (Acts 2:23).

In reality, legalists are not much different from antinomians, if indeed they are different at all. Pharisaic selective obedience is disobedience. Oliver O'Donovan perceptively notes that legalism and antinomianism are in fact two sides of the same coin because they are "fleshly" ways of living life. Christian ethics is not a matter of finding a middle ground between

2. As the Particular Baptist theologian Andrew Fuller remarked in his work against Antinomianism: "The name signifies that which is contrary to the law; because those who are denominated Antinomians profess to renounce the moral law as a rule of conduct, and maintain that as believers in Christ they are delivered from it. This appellation, so far as it goes, seems to be appropriate; but it is far from expressing all the distinguishing opinions of which the system is composed." Andrew Fuller, *Antinomianism Contrasted With the Religion Taught and Exemplified in the Holy Scriptures in The Works of Andrew Fuller* (Edinburgh: Banner of Truth Trust, 2007), 338.

legalism and license. Rather, as O'Donovan notes, "such an approach could end up by being only what it was from the start, an oscillation between two sub-Christian forms of life. A consistent Christianity must take a different path altogether, the path of an integrally evangelical ethics which rejoices the heart and gives light to the eyes because it springs from God's gift to mankind in Jesus Christ."[3] According to O'Donovan, then, not only are legalism and antinomianism "fleshly" ways of approaching ethics, but also there can be no middle ground between these two realms since they are fundamentally the same error, albeit dressed up differently from case to case.[4] The grace of God in the person of Jesus Christ, properly understood, is the only solution to these twin heresies. In essence, the mistakes of legalism and antinomianism are Christological errors.

The following will be a brief survey of antinomian debates in the Reformation and post-Reformation eras, ending with the Marrow Controversy in the early eighteenth century. Many of the theological issues debated in these centuries are only given a cursory glance in this chapter. Subsequent chapters will give more detailed consideration to various questions that arise here. This chapter merely sets the stage for the rest of the book.

LUTHER AND THE LUTHERANS

During the Reformation, the doctrine of justification by faith alone was rediscovered. With its rediscovery, Protestantism emerged. Reformation and post-Reformation theologians held that there could never be union with Rome so long as she insisted, as she still does today, that justification is not by faith alone. Historically, when a glorious truth is discovered, or even rediscovered, a number of half-truths or complete untruths are also birthed along with it. Not long after Martin Luther's (1483–1546) teaching on justification by faith alone had become public, one of his zealous disciples, Johann Agricola (c. 1494–1566), began to quarrel during the late 1520s with another one of Luther's disciples, the

---

3. Oliver O'Donovan, *Resurrection and Moral Order: An Outline for Evangelical Ethics* (Leicester: Apollos, 1996), 12.

4. Again, Fuller remarks: "It has been said that every unregenerate sinner has the heart of a Pharisee. This is true; and it is equally true that every unregenerate sinner has the heart of an Antinomian. . . . The quarrels between Antinomianism and Pharisaism arise, I think, more from misunderstanding than from any real antipathy between them." Fuller, *Antinomianism*, 338.

learned Philip Melanchthon (1497–1560), over questions relating to the law and the gospel.[5] At first, the principal issue between Melanchthon and Agricola was whether the preaching of the law was required for repentance and salvation. Agricola believed that the preaching of the gospel (and not the law) produced repentance, and that Melanchthon held an essentially Roman Catholic view. Luther would himself become embroiled in the controversy with Agricola, which resulted in Luther writing *Against the Antinomians* (1539).[6]

Luther was a colorful figure and had a penchant for hyperbole. His rhetoric is something to be admired, but not necessarily copied. He lived in remarkable times, when the theological landscape was constantly changing. So while his early enemies were the "papists," and they would remain so until he died, later he had to contend with the "false brethren" and various radical Protestants, including Agricola. His disputations with the latter caused him some grief, but Luther was never one to allow friendship to supersede the truth of God's Word. He coined the term "antinomian" in response to the excessive rhetoric against the law coming from those who supposedly belonged in his camp. Of course, the "softly singing Antinomians" (to use Luther's words) were a little bemused by his response to them. After all, Luther could be guilty of antinomian-sounding rhetoric himself. In fact, the hero of the English antinomian theologians in the seventeenth century was not Calvin, though he was cited by them (not infrequently out of context), but Luther. The seventeenth-century Scottish theologian Samuel Rutherford noted "how vainly Antinomians of our time boast that Luther is for them."[7]

David Como makes a telling statement in connection with this: "Luther confessed that some of his early writings had indeed stressed the notion that believers were free from the Law, but claimed that such excessive rhetoric had been necessary to deliver men from the bondage of papal works righteousness. 'Now, however, when the times are very dissimilar from those under the pope,' such rhetoric was no longer necessary, and if misunderstood, could lead men to an amoral, fleshly security

5. See Timothy J. Wengert, *Law and Gospel: Philip Melanchthon's Debate with John Agricola of Eisleben over Poenitentia* (Grand Rapids: Baker Books, 1997).

6. On Luther's debate with Agricola, see Mark U. Edwards, *Luther and the False Brethren* (Stanford: Stanford University Press, 1975), 156–79.

7. Samuel Rutherford, *A survey of the spirituall antichrist* (London, 1647), 1:69.

4

that threatened . . . moral and social order."[8] Luther was not only a man of his times, but a man who understood his times. Just as Paul's negative statements on the law typically arose from his conflict with Judaizers, so Luther's negative statements on the law must be understood in relation to his sixteenth-century opponents. His writings, even more so perhaps than the writings of any other figure in church history, must be historically located.[9] Context, in the case of statements made by Luther, is half the interpretation!

Interestingly, it seems that Luther would not have been surprised by his heroic status among later antinomian theologians. In his treatise *Against the Antinomians*, Luther comments that if he had died at Smalcald, he would have "forever been called the patron saint of such spirits [i.e., the antinomians], since they appeal to my books."[10] But Luther was no "antinomian"; that is, he was not against God's law—specifically, the Ten Commandments. Luther expounded the Ten Commandments in various places, sang them, and prayed them as well. In fact, he writes: "I know of no manner in which we do not use them, unless it be that we unfortunately do not practice and paint them with our deeds and our life as we should. I myself, as old and as learned as I am, recite the commandments daily word for word like a child."[11] As David Steinmetz acutely observes, Luther "does not reject good works except as the basis for justification. On the contrary, Luther wishes to stress as much as possible the importance of good works in the life of faith."[12] Likewise, Mark Edwards captures well Luther's objection to the antinomian preachers of his day, who were "fine Easter preachers but disgraceful Pentecost preachers, for they taught only redemption through Christ and not the sanctification through the Holy Spirit."[13] This particular criticism would resurface again, roughly a century later in Puritan England.

8. David Como, *Blown by the Spirit: Puritanism and the Emergence of an Antinomian Underground in Pre-Civil-War England* (Stanford: Stanford University Press, 2004), 113.
9. In his work on the moral law against the antinomians, the Puritan theologian Anthony Burgess showed that the emphases in Luther's earlier works were different from those in his later works. See Burgess, *Vindiciae legis: or, A vindication of the morall law and the covenants, from the Errours of Papists, Arminians, Socinians, and more especially Antinomians* (London: T. Underhill, 1646), 19–20.
10. Martin Luther, *Luther's Works*, ed. Jaroslav Pelikan and Helmut T. Lehmann, American Edition (Philadelphia: Muehlenberg and Fortress, and St. Louis: Concordia, 1955–86), 47:108.
11. Ibid., 47:109.
12. David C. Steinmetz, *Luther in Context*, 2nd ed. (Grand Rapids: Baker Academic, 2002), 119.
13. Edwards, *Luther and the False Brethren*, 170.

Antinomian debates among Lutheran theologians did not end with Luther's death in 1546. During the latter half of the sixteenth century, there were a number of tensions among Lutheran theologians relating to the law and the gospel.[14] Melanchthon, in fact, changed his view on repentance and agreed that the gospel was alone able to produce evangelical repentance. Perhaps even more controversially, he held to a "Reformed" view of the gospel, which included the whole doctrine of Christ, including repentance. The Gnesio-Lutherans disagreed with Melanchthon's view (i.e., the Philippist position) and defined the gospel narrowly as pure promise, which excluded repentance from consideration. Because he supposedly confused the law with the gospel, and argued that the gospel produced repentance, Melanchthon was accused of antinomianism. These debates show that among Lutheran theologians there were competing views on the law and the gospel, particularly in relation to the doctrine of repentance. And, in the midst of these debates, including the Majoristic Controversy, charges of antinomianism and popery were not infrequently used in order to get the upper hand.

ANTINOMIANISM IN PURITAN ENGLAND

The antinomian movement in England during the seventeenth century was in part a rebellion against Puritan piety and practice. It was also a theological movement that lacked the sophistication found in the writings of the best Reformed theologians. This lack of sophistication was a great cause of consternation among some Reformed divines, who frequently had to defend themselves against the charge of antinomianism from their Roman Catholic opponents. A further complication was the rising Arminian movement within Protestantism. The antinomians may have lacked the precision required to stay clear of various errors, while maintaining historic Reformed truths about *sola gratia*, but they were experts with their rhetoric—for they were the true defenders of free grace, or so they believed![15]

14. On this, see Martin Foord, "'A New Embassy': John Calvin's Gospel," in *Aspects of Reforming: Theology and Practice in Sixteenth Century Europe*, ed. Michael Parsons (Milton Keynes, UK: Paternoster, 2013), chap. 10. Incidentally, in this chapter Foord provides an excellent essay on Calvin's view of the law-gospel distinction.

15. See John Saltmarsh, *Free Grace* (London, 1645), and Robert Towne, *The Assertion of Grace* (London, 1645).

Studies of antinomianism in England during the seventeenth century have not always been kind to Puritan Reformed theologians. Como's impressively detailed study of antinomianism during this period suffers from some basic misunderstandings of Reformed theology and indeed the Bible itself, which is fairly common among social historians who make theological assessments. For example, he suggests that Puritanism "was a movement that attempted to preserve and reconcile the antinomian and the moralizing elements of the Pauline epistles."[16] John Coffey and Paul C. H. Lim make a valid claim about Puritan theology in relation to Luther's law-gospel schema, but they incorrectly accuse the Puritans of legalism: "And like the Reformed, they typically qualified Luther's antithesis between law and gospel, emphasising the role of God's law within the Christian life and the local community, and trying . . . to recreate godly Genevas in England and America. This legalism provoked an 'antinomian backlash' from within, but even when radical Puritans rejected orthodox Reformed ideas about the moral law or predestination or infant baptism, they still defined themselves in relation to the Reformed tradition."[17] Incidentally, noteworthy is the claim that the antinomians often viewed themselves as part of the Reformed theological tradition, not in opposition to it.

Scholars today who accuse the Puritans of legalism are simply echoing a pattern well established in the seventeenth century by antinomian theologians, who hurled the "legalist" epithet—as well as "crypto-papist" and the like—at those who were thoroughly Reformed in their theology. This was often a reaction against Reformed theologians who had described the theology of men like John Eaton (1574/5–1630/31), Tobias Crisp (1600–1643), John Saltmarsh (d. 1647), John Traske (c. 1585–1636), and Robert Towne (1592/3?–1664) as "antinomian." These theologians had different emphases and did not entirely agree with each other.

Therefore, the "antinomians" were not a monolithic group of theologians, but a group of theologians who were in error—sometimes serious—according to many orthodox divines.[18] Of course, the antinomian divines

---

16. Como, *Blown by the Spirit*, 130. Como's comments in the first paragraph of page 109, where he accuses Paul of contradicting himself, are similarly alarming.

17. John Coffey and Paul Chang-Ha Lim, eds., *The Cambridge Companion to Puritanism* (Cambridge: Cambridge University Press, 2008), 3.

18. There are typically problems when *-ism* is attached to a word, even in the case of "Puritanism." The Puritans were not a monolithic movement in terms of their theology. There were a number of

rejected the label that was imposed upon them. John Saltmarsh, for example, makes use of what was typically powerful rhetoric in the debate: "Can the Free-grace of Jesus Christ tempt any one to sin of itself? Can a good tree bring forth evil fruit? And shall we call every one Antinomian that speaks Free-grace, or a little more freely than we do?"[19] In other words, Saltmarsh and his friends essentially claimed that if to speak of "free grace" made them "antinomian," then they were guilty as charged. If the antinomian theologians evinced clever rhetoric in justifying themselves, the orthodox Reformed divines had a few tricks up their own sleeves too. Anthony Burgess (d. 1664), a prominent Puritan theologian, strongly asserted that the law cannot justify, which means that "we are all Antinomians in this sense."[20] But that was the only sense in which the orthodox could be "antinomian."

Those who criticized the antinomians were not fringe theologians who had been seduced by Arminian or Roman Catholic theology. No, they included the Westminster divines. A close reading of the Westminster documents reveals how opposed to antinomianism they were. Roman Catholicism, Arminianism, and Socinianism were major theological threats in England during the 1640s. But so too was antinomianism. Perhaps this was the case because of what antinomian theology might lead to, rather than what in fact it was. Even so, stalwart Reformed theologians such as Thomas Goodwin (1600–1680), Thomas Gataker (1574–1654), Samuel Rutherford (c. 1600–1661), Thomas Shepard (1605–49), and John Flavel (bap. 1630, d. 1691), some of whom had international reputations, wrote copiously on the errors of antinomians. Their polemical works on the subject reveal that the debate was more complicated than the question whether the moral law is still binding for Christians in the new covenant. The various debates involved the following questions:

1. Are there any conditions for salvation?
2. Is the moral law still binding for Christians?

Puritans who were not Reformed, for example. Equally, one has to affirm "shared characteristics" (see Como, *Blown by the Spirit*, 33–38) in order to speak of "antinomianism." But while there are dangers involved in this approach, lumping (as opposed to splitting) does have its advantages. Scholars have described the theology of certain individuals in England and New England during the seventeenth century as "antinomian," and so I will do likewise, even though there can be problems with such an approach.

19. Saltmarsh, *Free Grace*, "An Occasional Word."
20. Burgess, *Vindiciae legis*, 151.

3. What is the precise nature of, and relationship between, the law and the gospel?

4. Are good works necessary for salvation?

5. Does God love all Christians the same, irrespective of their obedience or lack thereof?

6. Who is the subject of spiritual activity, the believer or Christ?

7. May our assurance of justification be discerned by our sanctification?

8. Does God see sin in believers?

9. Is a person justified at birth or upon believing?[21]

These are some of the issues that were debated during the seventeenth century in England. The question of the abiding nature of the moral law was indeed central to the debate, but the other questions listed above were all related to that question. Debates on these issues were not taking place only in England. New England had to contend with many of the same questions.

ANTINOMIANISM IN NEW ENGLAND

While antinomian debates were raging in England from the 1630s to the 1650s, another antinomian controversy was taking place in New England. It involved (among others) a theologian (John Cotton), a politician (Henry Vane), and a laywoman (Anne Hutchinson). Michael P. Winship has shown that John Cotton (1585–1652) affirmed that "the dispute revolved around how to best magnify the free grace of God."[22] This dispute, which took place in the Massachusetts Bay Colony from 1636 to 1638, could be called the "free grace controversy," because it "seems both descriptively accurate and prejudicial to none of the actors."[23] This is a useful name, because antinomian debates have invariably been driven by the question of what it means to preach and teach the "free grace" of God.

Anne Hutchinson (bap. 1591, d. 1643) eventually came to the conclusion that only a few ministers were gospel preachers. The others, such as

---

21. This is my own list. Readers of Dutch may consult the sketch provided by G. A. van den Brink in *Herman Witsius en het antinomianisme: Met tekst en vertaling van de Animadversiones Irenicae* (Apledoorn: Instituut voor Reformatieonderzoek, 2008), 51n12.

22. Michael P. Winship, *Making Heretics: Militant Protestantism and Free Grace in Massachusetts, 1636–1641* (Princeton: Princeton University Press, 2002), 1.

23. Ibid.

Thomas Shepard and Thomas Hooker (1586?–1647), she thought, were basically legalists. One minister of whom Hutchinson approved was the well-known Congregationalist, John Cotton. Hutchinson's approval of Cotton only complicated matters for him. But, as Theodore Bozeman has noted, without Cotton's participation the "famed Antinomian Controversy of 1636–38 is difficult to imagine."[24] In fact, the controversy involved theologians from across the Atlantic as well. Cotton ended up writing a response to one of the Scottish commissioners at the Westminster Assembly, Robert Baillie (1602–62), who had accused him, among other things, of being antinomian.[25] Cotton staunchly denied the charge, but Hutchinson's approval of his ministry was enough evidence for those who were already suspicious of his theology. In his response to Baillie, the questions he answered, particularly on the relation of faith to union with Christ and justification, reveal the complexity of the debate. Cotton's view on the relation of faith to justification and union with Christ is highly technical. In short, he claimed that union with Christ takes place before the act of faith. Regeneration and union are roughly synonymous in his schema. As a result, because union precedes faith, so too does justification. But this is essentially an antinomian view, not the typical Reformed view that faith precedes justification.[26] Cotton, however, was fully aware of what he was doing when he departed from orthodox Reformed views, such as when he rejected faith as the instrumental cause of justification.

These questions were related to other theological issues that were being discussed at the time. With a clear eye on antinomian theology, the Synod of Elders, when Cotton was present, declared in 1637 that certain theological views were "unsafe." The "unsafe" propositions included the following statements from antinomian theologians:

1. To say we are justified by faith is an unsafe speech; we must say we are justified by Christ.
2. To evidence justification by sanctification or graces savours of Rome.

24. Theodore Dwight Bozeman, *The Precisianist Strain: Disciplinary Religion and Antinomian Backlash in Puritanism to 1638* (Chapel Hill: University of North Carolina Press, 2004), 241.

25. John Cotton, *The way of Congregational churches cleared* (London, 1648).

26. Cotton supposedly retracted his "antinomian" position after debate with the New England elders. See David D. Hall, *The Antinomian Controversy, 1636–1638: A Documentary History* (Durham, NC: Duke University Press, 1990), 411.

3. If I be holy, I am never the better accepted by God; if I be unholy, I am never the worse.

4. If Christ will let me sin, let him look to it; upon his honour be it.

5. Here is a great stir about graces and looking to hearts; but give me Christ; I seek not for graces, but for Christ . . . I seek not for sanctification, but for Christ; tell me not of meditation and duties, but tell me of Christ.

6. I may know I am Christ's, not because I do crucify the lusts of the flesh, but because I do not crucify them, but believe in Christ that crucified my lusts for me.

7. If Christ be my sanctification, what need I look to anything in myself, to evidence my justification?[27]

These statements get to the heart of the issues involved in the antinomian debates during the 1630s in New England—and indeed in England. They reveal that a century after Agricola's debates with Melanchthon and Luther, "antinomian" had taken on a new meaning.

NONCONFORMING ENGLAND

Even after the restoration of the monarchy in 1660, after the Civil War, the antinomian debates did not go away in England. In the 1690s, the controversy erupted between Presbyterians and Congregationalists. The highly respected Dutch theologian, Herman Witsius (1636–1708), played a role in this English nonconformist debate.[28] One of the things that set off the debate was the reprinting of Tobias Crisp's controversial sermons, *Christ Alone Exalted*. In the early 1640s, these sermons had caused a firestorm of controversy, and they did so again decades later by bringing Richard Baxter into the debate. Baxter's involvement was a little unfortunate for those who claimed to be orthodox, because his doctrine of justification was not orthodox. In fact, during these debates the term "neonomian" was coined by Isaac Chauncy (1632–1712) to describe Baxter. It appears that with a

27. Joseph B. Felt, *The Ecclesiastical History of New England* (Boston: Congregational Library Association, 1855–62), 1:318 ("Detrimental Speeches").

28. See Herman Witsius, *Conciliatory, or Irenical Animadversions, on the Controversies Agitated in Britain, under the unhappy names of Antinomians and Neonomians*, trans. Thomas Bell (Glasgow: W. Lang, 1807).

friend like Baxter on your side, enemies were unnecessary. Nonetheless, after Baxter died in 1691, his friend Daniel Williams (c. 1643–1716) became the leading spokesman against antinomian theology. Scholars have generally not been kind to Williams, but their negative assessments of his theology pale in comparison to the rhetoric that flowed from Isaac Chauncy's pen. Chauncy repeatedly referred to Williams as a "neonomian" because he spoke of the duties of the gospel as well as conditions for salvation. The specific point about "conditions" for salvation shows how complex the debates in the seventeenth century were.

As noted above, Baxter's involvement in the debate was not entirely helpful, because his peculiar theological beliefs—he was *sui generis*—meant he was also opposed by a perfectly orthodox theologian named John Owen (1616–83). Like Baxter and Williams, Owen was opposed to antinomianism, but, unlike Baxter, he was not a neonomian. Owen affirmed that there were conditions for salvation, which was what got Williams into trouble with Chauncy. But Owen was able to explain what he meant by conditions for salvation in a manner that was more precise and theologically sophisticated than the explanations of Williams.[29] Thus, the antinomian debates in the latter part of the seventeenth century revealed that just as there is a spectrum of antinomian theology (Saltmarsh vs. Crisp), so also is there a spectrum of neonomian theology (Baxter vs. Williams), as well as slight disagreement among orthodox theologians in expressing certain points of Reformed theology (Goodwin vs. Owen). It is far too simplistic and historically naïve to suggest that someone is antinomian only if he denies that the moral law has a place in the life of a believer. And it is likewise wrongheaded to suggest that "neonomians" are those who speak only of imperatives without the indicatives. In the seventeenth century, both antinomians and neonomians were typically reactionary theologians. Their reactions to the perceived excesses of certain groups were not always helpful or clearly articulated. For every John Owen or Thomas Manton, there was a Richard Baxter or a Tobias Crisp. The application for us today is really no different. In our zeal against errors and heresies, we are perhaps the

29. On Owen's opposition to antinomianism and his scholastic distinctions used in the debate, see Gert van den Brink, "Impetration and Application and John Owen's Theology," in *The Ashgate Research Companion to John Owen's Theology*, ed. Kelly M. Kapic and Mark Jones (Farnham, UK: Ashgate Publishing, 2012).

ones most vulnerable to infelicitous statements and hyperbolic rhetoric that often creates more heat than light.

THE MARROW

The sixteenth and seventeenth centuries were not the beginning and end of antinomian debates. In fact, perhaps the debate best known to present-day Christians on the topics of antinomianism and neonomianism (i.e., legalism) is the Marrow Controversy in the Church of Scotland from 1718 to 1726. Because of its close proximity to England, and because of the relatively short period of time between the English antinomian debates and the Marrow Controversy, as well as the fact that a certain book from England played such a significant role in the debate, the importance of the English context for the Scottish one cannot be overstated.

In 1645, a tract entitled *The Marrow of Modern Divinity* was published by Edward Fisher (b. 1611/12, d. 1656 or later), though only "E. F." appeared on the title page. Como records that *The Marrow* was a "minor bestseller," going through seven editions by 1650, but lost its public notoriety after the Restoration. However, seventy-three years after it was first published, "a Scotsman named Hog dusted off *The Marrow* and reissued it, occasioning a heated controversy that threatened to tear the Scottish Church in two. Defenders of the volume—so called 'Marrow Men'—claimed that the book represented a powerful practical exposition of the doctrine of grace. Its detractors saw it as a deceptive threat to the orthodoxy of the Church, a work of disguised antinomianism."[30]

Fisher's work was written as an attempted *via media* between the errors of antinomianism and legalism. Interestingly, however, Fisher's claims to be charting a middle ground did not impress his critics, either in the seventeenth or in the eighteenth centuries. Critics claimed that, if anything, *The Marrow* revealed Fisher's antinomian sympathies. The Presbyterian John Trapp (1601–69) actually called Fisher a "sly antinomian."[31] A number of scholars today tend to agree with that assessment, partly because Fisher

---

30. Como, *Blown by the Spirit*, 1.

31. See ibid., 4. James Buchanan remarks: "In regard to this question of fact, in the case of the 'Marrow,' we shall only say, that a book which is held even by its admirers to require explanatory or apologetic notes, may be fairly presumed to contain some unguarded expressions, which might be understood in a sense dangerous to some part of the scheme of divine truth; and that this remark applies equally to Fisher's 'Marrow of Modern Divinity,' which was annotated by Thomas Boston,

associated with antinomian ministers in the 1630s. Winship, for example, speaks of the "London barber who wrote the controversial antinomian-tinged *Marrow of Modern Divinity*."[32] In Scotland during the early eighteenth century, *The Marrow* would fall under similar condemnation by the Church of Scotland.

The controversy in Scotland involved many of the same issues that emerged in England and New England during the seventeenth century, but there were also new questions arising that previously had not been vigorously debated. The new issue that began the Marrow Controversy arose in 1717, when the Presbytery of Auchterarder required licentiates and ordinands to sign a series of propositions, one of which was: "I believe that it is not sound and orthodox to teach, that we must forsake sin in order to our coming to Christ, and instating us in covenant with God." According to the General Assembly, the Presbytery of Auchterarder had grievously erred, and a commission of the Assembly similarly disagreed with the proposition. As David Lachman notes, "it was in this context that *The Marrow* was republished and, on being attacked by Principal Hadow and defended by James Hog, became the occasion of controversy."[33]

The abovementioned proposition should never have been condemned by the General Assembly, but their condemnation and the resulting conflict show that legalism, flowering in the form of "hyper-Calvinism," was firmly entrenched in the Church of Scotland. As so often is the case, when one falls into error on one point of theology, other points necessarily follow. But those in the Church of Scotland who condemned the teachings of *The Marrow* firmly believed they were upholding Reformed orthodoxy against the incipient universalism of Edward Fisher. In other words, the Westminster Confession was (supposedly) defended by the opponents of *The Marrow*. One of the major points of contention in the debate was the phrase found in *The Marrow*, "Christ is dead for him." Interestingly, this phrase originally came from John Preston (1587–1628), who was an English hypothetical

---

and to Dr. Crisp's 'Sermons,' which were annotated by Dr. Gill." *The Doctrine of Justification* (Edinburgh: T&T Clark, 1867), 183.

32. Winship, *Making Heretics*, 57.

33. David C. Lachman, *The Marrow Controversy, 1718–1723: An Historical and Theological Analysis* (Edinburgh: Rutherford House, 1988), 7.

universalist.[34] Commenting on Preston's well-known phrase, Jonathan Moore suggests that Preston, "in common with all hypothetical universalists, explicitly grounded the universal call of the gospel, at least in part, in a universal aspect to Christ's satisfaction. . . . This is the language of hypothetical universalism and was identified as an error by some in Preston's circles, including the particular redemptionist Thomas Goodwin."[35] Thomas Boston (1676–1732) actually defended Preston's understanding of the Great Commission, but wrongly claimed that Preston held to particular redemption. Scholars such as Lachman have also adopted Boston's position that Preston was not a hypothetical universalist. Typically, particularist theologians wishing to defend Preston and Boston have tried to distinguish between "Christ died for you" and "Christ is dead for you." But, as Moore shows, Preston viewed these statements as roughly synonymous.[36]

Reformed theologians since John Calvin (1509–64) have actually disagreed on the nature of the free offer of the gospel.[37] Thomas Manton (bap. 1620, d. 1677) did not hold to the same position as John Owen, and John Preston's hypothetical universalism meant that his own view on the free offer of the gospel was also different from the positions of Owen and Manton. Opponents of the phrase "Christ is dead for him" were not wrong to pick up on the "universalism" of the statement, even if Fisher and Boston were thoroughgoing particularists. However, in reacting against that somewhat infelicitous phrase, the Scottish Assembly moved in the direction of hyper-Calvinism and legalism. As Boston and Hog correctly argued, the free offer of the gospel is not contingent upon the hearers meeting certain degrees of conviction. The Auchterarder Presbytery was correct to deny that Christians must forsake sin in order to come to Christ. After all, apart from Christ we can do nothing (John 15:5). But opponents of *The Marrow* believed that the elect are those who forsake sin, and therefore that grace is given to those people alone. In their view, one must forsake

---

34. See Jonathan D. Moore, *English Hypothetical Universalism: John Preston and the Softening of Reformed Theology* (Grand Rapids: Eerdmans, 2007).

35. Ibid., 117.

36. Ibid., 121.

37. See Martin Foord, "John Owen's Gospel Offer: Well-Meant or Not?" in *The Ashgate Research Companion to John Owen's Theology*, ed. Kapic and Jones. Foord claims that Owen holds essentially to a hyper-Calvinistic position on the gospel offer, as opposed to Thomas Manton.

sin in order to come to Christ.[38] In the preaching of the gospel, then, the benefits of Christ should only be offered to those for whom Christ died (i.e., the elect). But how do we know, in the preaching of the gospel, who it is for whom Christ died? The answer, according to the majority in the Church of Scotland: those who show enough contrition to receive Christ. The free offer became a conditional offer; Christ was divorced from his benefits; therefore, one could argue that this position was a Christological error more than anything else.

This specific debate during the Marrow Controversy sheds light on the nature of theological debates in which accusations of antinomianism and neonomianism are being made. First, unguarded phrases, either wrongly worded or wrongly understood, often lead to further unguarded ways of theologizing. Second, Boston was called an antinomian by legalists.[39] But just as Luther was no antinomian, so Boston was not one either. If Boston was guilty of anything, it was poor historical theology. All of this is to suggest that this brief historical survey reveals that hostile appellations in the context of theological debate are sometimes misplaced. But sometimes they are not. Just as there have been genuine legalists over the course of history, so too have there been genuine antinomians. But questions of who are genuine "antinomians" can only be answered by asking the right questions! By the end of this book, we hope to be able to set out the characteristics that justify someone being labeled an antinomian.

CONCLUSION

History has not always been kind to certain individuals. Nestorius (b. after 351; d. after 451) seems to have been one such figure, who lost the political battle and thus his claim to theological credibility. However, his archrival, Cyril of Alexandria (d. 444), had his flaws too. Centuries later, Martin Luther's discovery of the doctrine of justification by faith alone in the context of Roman Catholic legalism led him to speak about the law in ways that might raise a few eyebrows. There must be a reason, after all,

---

38. However, this is something that even Herman Witsius says, albeit he is speaking about the experience of the believer, which is not always how the *ordo salutis* is conceived. See *Conciliatory, or Irenical Animadversions*, 119–20.

39. See William VanDoodewaard's introductory essay in the modern reprint of Edward Fisher, *The Marrow of Modern Divinity* (Fearn, UK: Christian Focus Publications, 2009), 28–29.

why the English antinomians loved Luther so much. But whatever excessive language Luther may have used in some of the unguarded statements in his pre-1925 writings, he was not an antinomian in the sense of being against God's law. Likewise, John Cotton wrote and said things that were infelicitous, and he even constructed his view of union with Christ, justification, and faith in a way that was representative of antinomian thought. In general, however, Cotton was sound, but that did not mean he did not occasionally confuse others.

In seventeenth-century England, several prominent antinomian theologians were fiercely criticized. But one of them, Tobias Crisp, was defended by sound Reformed theologians, even centuries after his death. Likewise, Edward Fisher had his critics and his defenders, even among orthodox Reformed theologians. Indeed, he was not a theologian in the sense that John Owen and Francis Turretin were. They were far more sophisticated than Fisher, who had a sort of "Bunyan-esque" way about him. This might explain why *The Marrow*, while fitting within the bounds of Reformed orthodoxy, was nevertheless controversial. Also, despite the iconic status of the Marrow Men in Reformed circles, they were not guiltless in the debate that caused a firestorm of activity in the eighteenth century, even though they were heroic in the cause of truth. In other words, this short survey of debates over a few centuries has revealed that history is messy.

What hope is there, then, in coming to measured, sustainable conclusions about antinomianism? The answer depends on several factors. First, the right questions need to be asked. In contemporary Reformed circles, simply acknowledging and even affirming the "indicative-imperative" model will not suffice for guarding against legalism and antinomianism.[40] However important that model is—and I would say it is fundamental to the Christian faith—more specific questions need to be addressed, which will be a central focus of later chapters in this book. Second, Christology will always prove to be decisive in debates on antinomianism. In relation to the questions that are being asked, the answers must always have a Christological focus. A Reformed view of Christ's person is as important as a Reformed view of his work in this whole issue. The general neglect and subordination of

---

40. This phrase is now a theological commonplace in Reformed circles, referring to what God has done (indicative) and what we are commanded to do (imperative). The phrase itself would be anachronistic if attributed to seventeenth-century Reformed divines, but the concept is clearly present in their writings.

Christ's person to his work in many circles today has, as it did in the past, disastrous consequences for theology. Antinomianism is fundamentally a Christological problem (a point I intend to defend), as much as it is a problem of the heart and mind. Third, the importance of historical theology to the tasks of exegetical and systematic theology cannot go unnoticed. A number of errors that are popular today have been addressed before, and with great clarity. But resurrected errors require resurrected answers that build on and clarify Reformed orthodoxy. There are indeed areas for disagreement and debate within the Reformed tradition, as I have pointed out elsewhere.[41] But there are views that simply fall outside the bounds of Reformed orthodoxy. Even more importantly, they cannot be sustained by the Scriptures. Finally, as this chapter has shown, the term "antinomianism" is a lot more complex than its etymology might suggest. The following chapters will reveal that acknowledging a place for the moral law in the life of the believer may not be sufficient if other truths are either neglected (as is often the case) or denied (as is sometimes the case).

41. See Michael A. G. Haykin and Mark Jones, eds., *Drawn into Controversie: Reformed Theological Diversity and Debates within Seventeenth-Century British Puritanism* (Göttingen: Vandenhoeck & Ruprecht, 2011).

2

THE IMITATION OF CHRIST

"FOR TO THIS YOU HAVE BEEN CALLED,
BECAUSE CHRIST ALSO SUFFERED FOR YOU,
LEAVING YOU AN EXAMPLE, SO THAT YOU
MIGHT FOLLOW IN HIS STEPS." —1 PETER 2:21

JESUS CHRIST, in his human nature, is the holiest man ever to have lived on earth. He exercised faith, hope, and love in a manner so extraordinary that if there were millions of worlds of loving creatures, they would not have, combined together, the same degree of love that was in the heart of our Savior. These graces bestowed upon Jesus did not remain on him alone, but trickled down, as oil on his forehead, to his bride.[1] "And from his fullness we have all received, grace upon grace" (John 1:16).

Discussions and writings on holiness often lack a strong Christological basis and center. Without a robust affirmation of the holiness of Christ, and all that that means, calls to holiness, however stirring they may be, will inevitably devolve into a form of man-centered pietism. In the case of our Lord, his graces were put to the test over the course of his life, as he learned obedience through suffering (Heb. 5:7–10). The one who is perfect was made perfect. As the Puritan theologian Thomas Goodwin memorably comments in his work on gospel holiness, "The heart of Christ had an ocean of love naturally flowing in it, and yet he must learn mercy

---

1. Although Christ did not require grace in terms of forgiveness of sin, he was filled with all of the gifts and graces of the Holy Spirit needed to have all human perfections.

and pity to us, in a way of [experience]" (Heb. 2:18).[2] Learning what holiness is, and how holiness is accomplished, is thoroughly Christocentric. The post-Reformation scholar Richard Muller has questioned the usefulness of labeling various theologians over the centuries as "Christocentric," mostly because no theologian would claim not to be Christocentric.[3] And when theologians from various theological traditions all make the claim to be Christocentric, there is perhaps good reason to question the value of the term. Nonetheless, the truth is that not all books on holiness have adequately thought through the person and work of Christ in relation to his holiness and the holiness of believers. If Reformed theologians have typically held to a distinctive view of Christ's person, which I believe is the case, especially among the English Puritans, then Reformed theologians should necessarily hold to a distinctive view on holiness.

CHRIST THE CENTER

The Scriptures are clear that God's holiness provides the reason why humans made in his image should be holy. When Peter exhorts his fellow believers in Christ to be holy because God is holy, he does so on the basis of what was written in the past (see 1 Peter 1:16; Lev. 11:44; 19:2; 20:7). This is a point that hardly needs defending, and it is a basic point that was made by the great Reformed theologians of the past.[4] It shows that if Christians can have any enjoyable communion with God, it must be a holy enjoyment based on the holiness of both parties. Having said that, the so-called prince of the Puritans, John Owen, makes an important Christological point in connection with the holiness of God. He notes that God's holiness, as one of his essential attributes, "is not the immediate ground of and motive unto holiness; but it is the holiness of God as manifested and revealed unto us in Christ Jesus."[5] God's infinite, eternal holiness would be too much for us to bear if he related to us only on those terms. As sinful creatures, we

---

2. Thomas Goodwin, *The Works of Thomas Goodwin, D.D.* (1861–66; repr., Grand Rapids: Reformation Heritage Books, 2006), 7:137.

3. Richard A. Muller, "A Note on 'Christocentrism' and the Imprudent Use of Such Terminology," *Westminster Theological Journal* 68 (2006): 253–60.

4. See Peter van Mastricht, *Theoretico-practica theologia, qua, per singula capita Theologica, pars exegetica, dogmatica, elenchtica & practica, perpetua successione conjugantur,* new ed. (Amsterdam, 1724), 201, 206–7.

5. John Owen, *The Works of John Owen, D.D.,* ed. William H. Goold (Edinburgh: Johnstone & Hunter, 1850–55), 3:570.

are unable to answer with our own holiness to the holiness of God, that is, apart from God's covenantal condescension.[6] Owen remarks that "it is the holiness of God as he is in Christ, and as in Christ represented unto us, that gives us both the necessity and motive unto ours."[7] If Christ is our mediator, our union with him means not only that we must be holy (i.e., necessity), but also that we will be able to be like him (i.e., motive) and, of course, that we will enjoy being holy (i.e., communion).[8]

The grace that we need for our sanctification is indeed the grace of God. But it is the grace of God in and through his Son, Jesus Christ, by the grace of the Holy Spirit (2 Cor. 13:14). In other words, whatever grace we receive for our holiness first belonged to the Savior (John 1:16). As the resurrected Lord of the new creation, Christ has exclusive right to this prerogative (Col. 1). His headship is not only of "power and rule, but of life and influence."[9] Thus, God "communicates nothing that belongs properly to the covenant of grace, as our sanctification and holiness do, unto any, but in and through him. And we receive nothing by him but by virtue of relation unto him, or especial interest in him, or union with him."[10] Christ is not only, "morally considered, the most perfect, absolute, glorious pattern of all grace, holiness, virtue, obedience, to be chosen and preferred above all others, but he only is so; there is no other complete example of it."[11] Whatever problems people may have with the concept of the *imitatio Christi* (imitation of Christ), we cannot escape the reality that if we have any interest in Christ, we must emulate him in his holiness.[12]

Again, Owen notes that faith in Christ for redemption, which includes justification and sanctification, is only half of our duty of faith, which has in view Christ's atoning death for our sins that gives us peace with God, reconciliation, and the imputation of his righteousness. In Owen's words, "Unto these ends, indeed, is he firstly and principally proposed unto us in

---

6. On God's covenantal condescension, see the excellent work of Scott K. Oliphint, *God with Us: Divine Condescension and the Attributes of God* (Wheaton, IL: Crossway, 2012).

7. Owen, *Works*, 3:570.

8. Chapters 1 and 7 of John Owen's treatise on the mortification of sin (*Works*, vol. 6) deal with union with Christ. This is the centerpiece of his work on sanctification, but readers sometimes miss this vital point because they are consumed with the "how to" of Christian living.

9. Owen, *Works*, 3:414.

10. Ibid.

11. Ibid., 3:510.

12. See Sinclair B. Ferguson's comments on this point in *The Holy Spirit* (Downers Grove, IL: InterVarsity Press, 1996), 152–53.

the gospel, and with respect unto them are we exhorted to receive him and believe in him; but this is not all that is required of us. Christ in the gospel is proposed unto us as our pattern and example of holiness; and as it is a cursed imagination that this was the whole end of his life and death,—namely, to exemplify and confirm the doctrine of holiness which he taught,—so to neglect his so being our example, in considering him by faith to that end, and labouring after conformity to him, is evil and pernicious."[13] Owen does not here explicitly name the antinomians of his day, but there is little doubt that he is critiquing their penchant for disregarding Christ as our example of what personal holiness should look like. Of course, Owen is careful here to note that Christ's works of impetration (e.g., death on the cross) are "principally proposed" to us, but to neglect Christ as our pattern of holiness is nevertheless "evil and pernicious." Impetration—not a concept that is well known to readers today—has in view Christ's meritorious work; application refers to the enjoyment of Christ's purchase of redemption. The two concepts are distinct, but not separate.[14] So to be holy is both to look to Christ's work of reconciliation (i.e., impetration) and to labor after conformity to his image (Eph. 1:4; Rom. 8:29). The following questions must therefore be asked: How and in what power was Christ made holy? And what relation does his own pattern of holiness have to his people?

CHRIST'S LIFE OF FAITH

Jesus of Nazareth was no ordinary man. He was the God-man, without spot, stain, or wrinkle in his human nature. But he still had a human nature, and because the finite cannot comprehend the infinite (*finitum non capax infiniti*), there was room for real advancement in his human nature.

---

13. Owen, *Works*, 3:513.

14. With respect to salvation, John Owen distinguishes between impetration and application in the following way: "By impetration we mean the meritorious purchase of all good things made by Christ for us with and of his Father; and by application, the actual enjoyment of those good things upon our believing;—as, if a man pay a price for the redeeming of captives, the paying of the price supplies the room of the impetration of which we speak; and the freeing of the captives is as the application of it. Yet, then, we must observe, That all the things which Christ obtained for us are not bestowed upon condition, but some of them absolutely. And as for those that are bestowed upon condition, the condition on which they are bestowed is actually purchased and procured for us, upon no condition but only by virtue of the purchase. For instance. Christ hath purchased remission of sins and eternal life for us, to be enjoyed on our believing, upon the condition of faith. But faith itself, which is the condition of them, on whose performance they are bestowed, that he hath procured for us absolutely, on no condition at all." *Works*, 10:223–24.

He knew no sin in his own experience, and the unity of his person—he is one person with two distinct natures—meant that he was unable to sin.[15] Nevertheless, while he lived on earth during his state of humiliation, he lived by faith, not by sight. Because Christ is the holiest man ever to have lived, he is the greatest believer ever to have lived (Heb. 12:2). There has never been, nor will there ever be, a more perfect example of living by faith than Jesus. Reformed theologians have historically agreed—though, I fear, we have lost this precious truth today—that Christ had faith for justification (i.e., vindication, Isa. 50:8). Of course, unlike us, he did not need to go through a mediator to be justified by his Father, for he was not ungodly like us (cf. Rom. 4:5). But he still needed justification, which culminated at his resurrection (1 Tim. 3:16), because of his accursed death (Gal. 3:13). By faith, he believed the word and promises of God. Furthermore, Christ did not exercise faith merely for himself; he also exercised faith for all those for whom he died, so that they may receive from him that particular grace. For there is no grace we receive that was not first present in Christ himself, particularly the grace of faith. As Richard Sibbes notes, "We must know that all things are first in Christ, and then in us."[16]

The life of holiness is therefore the life of faith. The way we begin the Christian life is the way we continue in the Christian life until we get to heaven, where faith becomes sight. If that was required for the sinless Lamb of God, how much more so for us, who have remaining indwelling sin?

As Jesus lived by faith, he also perfectly kept God's commandments. He remained in the Father's love because he kept his commandments (John 15:10). The importance of Christ's life of faith and obedience as an example for our own life is wonderfully illustrated in Hebrews 10:38–39.[17] Many commentators miss the rather salient point that this verse applies not only to believers, but especially to Jesus Christ. Christ is the righteous one who lives by faith (cf. Heb. 2:13), and if he had shrunk back (i.e., sinned) just

---

15. I have elsewhere written on the person of Christ and questions related to his natures, temptations, etc. See Mark Jones, *A Christian's Pocket Guide to Jesus Christ: An Introduction to Christology* (Fearn, UK: Christian Focus Publications, 2012).

16. Richard Sibbes, *The Works of the Reverend Richard Sibbes* (Aberdeen: J. Chalmers, 1809), 1:103. Sibbes's "Description of Christ" is one of the finest treatments of the person of Christ in relation to the Holy Spirit and Christ's graces that I have found anywhere.

17. "'But my righteous one shall live by faith, and if he shrinks back, my soul has no pleasure in him.' But we are not of those who shrink back and are destroyed, but of those who have faith and preserve their souls."

once, God would have had no pleasure in him. But through our union with Christ, "we are not of those who shrink back and are destroyed, but of those who have faith and preserve their souls" (Heb. 10:39). In the life of the believer, then, faith is the instrumental cause of their sanctification. Without faith, there is no possibility of holiness (Acts 15:9).

THE SPIRIT AND CHRIST

Discussions of sanctification should always have a rich pneumatological element. Books over the ages have to varying degrees been successful in relating the Holy Spirit to the believer in the life of holiness. What has not always received adequate attention, however, is the work of the Spirit on Christ in relation to his holiness as the pattern for our own. In one respect, this is understandable, but in another, it is entirely unacceptable. When certain Reformed pastors and theologians speak of Christ being "placed under a covenant of works" (as the second Adam), we might be tempted to think that Christ was left to his own abilities to obey the law of God for us. Without question, the obedience offered by Christ from the cradle to the grave was his obedience. But he was obedient in the power of the Holy Spirit. He never uttered a kind word, nor thought a good thought, except in reliance upon the Spirit of holiness. There was a perfect synergy involved in Jesus' human obedience and the Holy Spirit's influence as he "increased in wisdom and in stature and in favor with God and man" (Luke 2:52). A careful analysis of Christ's life reveals that at the most significant points in it (e.g., his conception, birth, baptism, preaching ministry, death, and resurrection) the Holy Spirit was present, enabling him in all that he was required to do.

Following this pattern, those who belong to Christ are as dependent upon the Spirit for their holiness as they are dependent upon air to breathe. Although man is completely passive at the moment of regeneration, he cooperates with God in sanctification. As noted above, Christ's obedience was truly his own. His own faculties were involved, but that does not mean that *only* his faculties were involved. He, like us, relied upon the Holy Spirit for his holiness (Isa. 11:2). But exactly what this looks like is the crux of the issue. In his brilliant treatment of the Spirit's relation to Christ's human nature, Owen addresses this question:

The Lord Christ, as man, did and was to exercise all grace by the rational faculties and powers of his soul, his understanding, will, and affections; for he acted grace as a man. . . . His divine nature was not unto him in the place of a soul, nor did [the divine nature] immediately operate the things which he performed, as some of old vainly imagined; but being a perfect man, his rational soul was in him the immediate principle of all his moral operations, even as ours are in us. . . . [Christ's] growth in grace and wisdom was the peculiar work of the Holy Spirit; for as the faculties of his mind were enlarged by degrees and strengthened, so the Holy Spirit filled them up with grace for actual obedience.[18]

Owen's points above have significant ramifications for the issue of antinomianism. In short, he notes that Christ's divine nature did not act immediately upon him during his life on earth. Instead, the divine nature operated upon his human nature mediately by the Holy Spirit, who enabled him to exercise the rational faculties that were proper to his human nature. His mind and heart, for example, received the grace of the Holy Spirit. In the same way, our souls are the immediate principle of our moral actions, but our morally righteous actions are impossible apart from the grace of the Holy Spirit strengthening us for actual obedience.

THE SPIRIT IN THE BELIEVER

In New England, there was a debate regarding the nature of sanctification between Anne Hutchinson and her sympathizers, on the one hand, and the orthodox elders, such as Thomas Shepard, on the other. No one disagreed that our holiness is entirely from God. In fact, even Pelagius taught this truth, albeit with a gross inconsistency. The debate focused on two related points of divinity, namely, how the Spirit of Christ enables believers to perform acts of holiness and the nature of Christ's substitution for believers. As William K. Stoever notes, "Shepard and his colleagues maintained that sanctification consists primarily in habits infused, in powers enabling, and in a gracious disposition inclining to holy acts, rather than in acts *qua* acts."[19] According to Stoever, the debate had to do with how holiness is present in the believer, whether "inherently, or accidentally

18. Owen, *Works*, 3:169–70.
19. William K. Stoever, *"A Faire and Easie Way to Heaven": Covenant Theology and Antinomianism in Early Massachusetts* (Middletown, CT: Wesleyan University Press, 1978), 68.

and immediately from Christ."[20] The orthodox affirmed the former (i.e., "inherently"), whereas the antinomians typically affirmed the latter (i.e., "accidentally" and "immediately").

Because the antinomians, both in England and New England, desired to limit (sometimes completely) human activity in the life of the believer, they basically held to a radical form of substitution between the believer and Christ. Christ, not the believer, acted. In England, Tobias Crisp seemed to be arguing for this same view. He claimed that if a man is in Christ, then "Christ does all his work for him, as well as in him. . . . Christ does all for them, that God requires of them to be done."[21] Unguarded statements like this—and Crisp was famous for overstating truths to the point where they became stumbling blocks—were one of the primary reasons why the Westminster divines were so worried about his theology. Gert van den Brink accurately claims that "conversion, sorrow, faith, sanctification, or any other part of the order of salvation in which human activity seems to be necessary is interpreted by the antinomians in substitutionary ways."[22]

In connection with this way of understanding the relation of Christ and the Spirit to believers, the New England elders rightly argued that the Spirit of Christ did not act for believers immediately, but "mediately, by created graces [e.g., love] infused into the soul, which empower the person himself to act."[23] What must be guarded against is the idea that since Christ performed everything as our representative in his works of impetration, he likewise carries out the actions of believers in the application of redemption.[24] Redemption necessarily involves application, but application cannot be swallowed up by impetration, so that the believer is practically absolved of any responsibility for his actions, whether good or bad ones. If the antinomians are correct to insist on the "immediate actings of the

20. Ibid.

21. Tobias Crisp, *Christ alone exalted, being the compleat works of Tobias Crisp, D.D., containing XLII sermons* (London, 1690), 124. Many thanks to Gert van den Brink for bringing this section of Crisp's sermons to my attention.

22. G. A. van den Brink, "Calvin, Witsius (1636–1708) and the English Antinomians," in *The Reception of John Calvin and His Theology in Reformed Orthodoxy*, ed. Andreas J. Beck and William den Boer (Leiden: Brill, 2011), 232–33.

23. Stoever, *"A Faire and Easie Way,"* 68.

24. Similarly, Herman Bavinck suggests that antinomianism is "the trend that reduces the application of salvation to its acquisition and almost completely equates the two. On this view, Christ has accomplished everything." *Reformed Dogmatics*, vol. 3, *Sin and Salvation in Christ*, trans. John Vriend (Grand Rapids: Baker, 2006), 530.

Spirit," then, according to Thomas Shepard, "there is seeing in a Christian without an eye, and hearing without an ear, and knowing Christ without an understanding, and loving without love, and living without life."[25] According to this view, the Christian does not in fact act or do anything himself.[26] Thus, the antinomians take the truth that Christ achieved perfect obedience on behalf of the believer—what is commonly referred to as the active obedience of Christ—and wrongly deduce that when the believer performs any act, it is actually Christ doing so immediately by his Spirit. Shepard elsewhere notes the antinomian conflation of justification and sanctification, whereby "mortification and vivification are nothing but a believing that Christ hath mortified sin for them."[27] The antinomians essentially "confound" justification and sanctification and insist that true sanctification is nothing but believing the gospel more and more. Moreover, if any positive change takes place in the believer, it is because "Christ hath mortified sin for them."[28]

Incidentally, this issue was also a point of contention that emerged between John Flavel and the Baptist theologian Philip Cary in their debate over the proper subjects of baptism.[29] In short, these men disagreed on whether the new covenant had conditions or not. Flavel argued that faith is properly a condition of the new covenant, and was charged by Cary with sneaking a covenant of works into the new covenant. Flavel responded by noting that the faith that God requires is a gift, which answers the charge of bringing a covenant of works into the Christian life. Following from that, Flavel makes a crucial distinction between power and act:

> This is a mistake, and the mistake in this leads you into all the rest; though faith (which we call the condition on our part) be the gift of God, and the power of Believing be derived from God; yet the act of believing is properly our act . . . else it would follow, when we act any grace, as Faith,

25. Thomas Shepard, *The parable of the ten virgins opened & applied, being the substance of divers sermons on Matth. 25, 1–13 wherein the difference between the sincere Christian and the . . . hypocrite . . . are clearly discovered* (London, 1660), 178. See also Samuel Rutherford, *A survey of the spirituall antichrist* (London, 1647), 2:53–56.

26. Cf. Como, *Blown by the Spirit*, 37.

27. Thomas Shepard, *Theses Sabatticae*, in *The Works of Thomas Shepard* (Boston: Doctrinal Tract and Book Society, 1853), 3:92.

28. Ibid., 3:92.

29. On this debate, see Joel R. Beeke and Mark Jones, *A Puritan Theology: Doctrine for Life* (Grand Rapids: Reformation Heritage Books, 2012), 725–41.

> Repentance, or Obedience, that God believes, repents, and obeys in us,
> and it is not we, but God that does all of these.[30]

So the conditional aspect of the covenant of grace must be understood in relation to divine causality and "the liberty or contingency of second causes" (WCF 3.1). The divine element and human responsibility are upheld by Flavel, which is something that not only Cary failed to do, but also the majority of antinomian theologians. Faith is therefore both the gift of God and the act of man.

Pastorally, the implications of any view are crucial. Heresy and error always have practical consequences. While certain preachers may reject the basic structure of the antinomian view described above, their failure to exhort people to "love your neighbor" (Mark 12:31), "pray" (1 Thess. 5:25), "stand firm" (2 Thess. 2:15), and "resist the devil" (James 4:7), for example, is a practical affirmation of the view that Christ is the subject of spiritual activity in the believer. Incidentally, the common assertion, "You just need to believe the gospel more," essentially undermines the position of the antinomian, not least because it devolves into a sometimes oppressive and monotonous mantra that takes the place of the multifaceted exhortations one finds in the Scriptures. Consistency would demand that if Christ works only immediately by his Spirit, then our preaching should actually be aimed directly at Christ and not at the congregation! But the Scriptures are clear. David's words in Psalm 51:10 ("Create in me a clean heart, O God, and renew a right spirit within me") show that God's work of holiness does not bypass the moral faculties of the believer, but rather renews them and purifies them (by faith in the power of the Spirit) in order for the believer to use his own God-given (and now God-restored) faculties.

CONCLUSION

In keeping with the general tenor of this book, the purpose of this chapter has not been to provide a full picture of the life of holiness.[31] Rather, a number of points have been made in order to clarify the problem of anti-

---

30. John Flavel, *The Works of the Rev. Mr. John Flavel* (1820; repr., Edinburgh: Banner of Truth, 1997), 6:352–53.

31. For example, I have not discussed the "negative" side of holiness, mortification (Rom. 8:13). On this, see Owen's well-known treatise on mortification in his *Works*, 6:5–86.

nomianism. First, the issue that confronted broadly Reformed churches was not whether we are dependent upon God and his grace for our holiness. Both orthodox and antinomian theologians agreed that holiness is impossible apart from the grace of God. Indeed, they both agreed that the saints are completely, not partly, dependent upon the grace of God. To deny the necessity of the Holy Spirit for our inherent righteousness is to deny the gospel. Second, the example of Christ has been highlighted in order to show that Christ's own holiness, including the means by which he was made holy, is not unrelated to our own pattern of holiness. Our great act of faith brings us to focus on Christ's mediatorial work for us. His life, death, resurrection, ascension, and intercession are the grounds for the holiness of his people. For that reason, our holiness is simply the implanting of the gospel in our defiled souls. But our life of faith also focuses on Christ as our example of holiness. Third, with this focus in mind, the difference between the antinomians and the orthodox on this point has to do with the mechanism of how God sanctifies his people. Just as Christ lived by faith and depended upon the grace of the Holy Spirit to work on his human nature, so we are likewise to live by faith and depend upon the Holy Spirit to enable us to love God with all of our heart, soul, mind, and strength. But our holiness is not the immediate acting of Christ's Spirit, as though he were the only actor. We have not been deprived of our wills; rather, the Spirit makes our hearts and minds able to do God's will (Phil. 2:13).

The antinomians did not, then, as the last chapter showed, simply argue against the continuing role of the moral law in the life of the believer. Rather, they attempted to blur the distinction between impetration and application, and so make Christ totally responsible, not only for our imputed righteousness, but also for our imparted righteousness. On the surface, such a view appears to honor Christ. But on closer inspection, this view obliterates human responsibility to the point that antinomianism ends up becoming a form of hyper-Calvinism.

As David Como has shown, there were two forms of antinomianism in seventeenth-century England, the "imputative" and the "perfectionist" (or "inherentist") strains.[32] Without wanting to minimize the differences

---

32. Como, *Blown by the Spirit*, 38–40. Readers will note that the imputative strain is given more attention in this book. Indeed, most historical treatments of antinomianism, whether recent or from the seventeenth century, include mention of Gnostics and mystics, sometimes known as "Familists"

between these two strains, there is the fascinating oddity that the strong imputative view, when joined with pneumatology, actually has the potential to morph into a form of perfectionism whereby people are told that there is too much of themselves and not enough of Christ. Human responsibility is practically obliterated by Christ's "responsibility." The imputation of Christ's obedience for our justification does not mean that our holiness is all Christ's and not our own. One should note, of course, that in Galatians 2:19–20 the word "I" appears more often than the word "Christ."[33]

(e.g., see Como, *Blown by the Spirit*, 4–9, 38–53). Also, Samuel Rutherford traces antinomianism back to the mystics (*Spirituall antichrist*, part 1, passim).

33. "I have been crucified with Christ. It is no longer I who live, but Christ who lives in me. And the life I now live in the flesh I live by faith in the Son of God, who loved me and gave himself for me."

3

THE LAW

"THE THIRD, AND PRINCIPAL USE, WHICH
PERTAINS MORE CLOSELY TO THE PROPER
USE OF THE LAW, FINDS ITS PLACE AMONG
BELIEVERS IN WHOSE HEARTS THE SPIRIT
OF GOD ALREADY LIVES AND REIGNS."
—JOHN CALVIN[1]

THE ROLE OF "THE LAW" in the life of the Christian has historically been one of the most difficult and contentious points in divinity. It
was the preeminent issue during the antinomian crisis in England from the
1620s to the 1640s. As noted in chapter 1, antinomianism in England and
New England in the seventeenth century was not easily defined because
of the range of views among antinomians and the fact that even otherwise
orthodox Reformed theologians sometimes entertained views that were
typically associated with antinomianism.[2] Despite the complexity of the
whole antinomian movement, there was nonetheless, according to David
Como, "a propensity to argue that the Mosaic Law, including the Decalogue,
was in some sense abolished, abrogated, or superseded for Christians."[3] In

1. John Calvin, *Institutes of the Christian Religion*, ed. John T. McNeill, trans. Ford Lewis Battles
(Philadelphia: Westminster Press, 1960), 2.7.12.
2. Chad van Dixhoorn, "The Strange Silence of Prolocutor Twisse: Predestination and Politics in
the Westminster Assembly's Debate over Justification," *Sixteenth Century Journal* 40 (2009): 395–418.
3. David Como, *Blown by the Spirit: Puritanism and the Emergence of an Antinomian Underground
in Pre-Civil-War England* (Stanford: Stanford University Press, 2004), 34.

Como's view, the chief characteristic that defined the Stuart antinomians was their view that they were free from the Mosaic code. This point needs to be clarified, however, since orthodox theologians from the Reformed tradition also could affirm that position, albeit with the requisite qualifications and distinctions.

Interestingly, Como draws attention to what he perceives to be obvious inconsistencies in the Scriptures on this issue—between Paul and James, for example. Paul inherited an "unstructured but authentic anti-legal spirit from the early Christ movement," and thus his statements on the law were "improvisations of his own making." In fact, Paul's radical views on the law were "not obviously or unambiguously in line with the teaching of Jesus," which meant that James and Peter "recoiled at Paul's wholesale rejection of the Law as an inauthentic corruption of their master's teaching."[4] In the end, according to Como, Christ's followers were unable to agree on the role of the law in the life of a Christian. Those of a Reformed persuasion may not appreciate Como's pitting of Paul against James and Peter, but we should have some sympathy for his awareness of the complexity of the issue. And Como is not alone. New Testament scholars such as Heikki Räisänen have expressed similar sentiments.[5] To that list could be added literally hundreds of scholars who have argued for views on the law that would be sympathetic to the antinomian view that the Decalogue has been abolished and no longer continues as a rule for Christians.

This chapter deals with some of these concerns. But the questions addressed will focus on specific issues having to do with the commanding nature of the moral law in the new covenant, not whether the Decalogue, as given to Moses, remains in force for the Christian today. Even among orthodox Reformed theologians in the post-Reformation era, there were different views on how best to speak of the nature of the moral law in the new covenant. Divines such as Girolamo Zanchi (1516–90) and André Rivet (1572–1651) did not hold that the moral law as given by Moses was binding on Christians. Anthony Burgess, in his classic defense of the moral law, *Vindiciae legis*, affirms that "there are some learned and solid Divines, as Zanchy and Rivet . . . which hold the Law, as delivered by Moses, not

---

4. Ibid., 106–7.
5. Heikki Räisänen, *Paul and the Law* (Philadelphia: Fortress, 1986).

to belong to us."[6] However, Burgess is careful to note, and rightly so, that these theologians are "expressly against the Antinomists: for they say, that howsoever the Law does not bind under that notion, as Mosaical; yet it binds, because it is confirmed by Christ: so that although the first obligation ceases, and we have nothing to do with Moses now; yet the second obligation, which comes by Christ, is still upon us."[7] Clearly, the antinomians were saying things far more radical than what one finds in the writings of Zanchi and Rivet.

SIC ET NON [YES AND NO]

Perhaps the defining issue between the orthodox and the antinomians was not whether the moral law plays a role in justification *coram Deo*, but whether the moral law has any positive role in the salvation of believers. Or so the argument goes. Writing against the antinomians, Henry Burton (1578–1648) claims that they deny any use at all of the moral law: "They allow the law no further use, than as to be a School-master to bring us to Christ, and then farewell law."[8] They not only commit sins of omission, but heighten the problem by railing against ministers who "press the duties of sanctification."[9] Interestingly, Burton adds: "I should not have believed there had been such mouths of blasphemy in the world, had not mine ears been witnesses of them."[10] Como agrees that, from this perspective, the use of the law, while still of some value to the believer, is "primarily negative."[11] For the antinomians, the law "served, in short, to remind them how lucky they were to be free of it."[12]

As is often the case in debates of this nature, the orthodox faced an almost insuperable problem, namely, that the antinomians spoke out of both sides of their mouths. A close reading of antinomian writings from the seventeenth century shows that they were not always clear. Ambiguity was a hallmark of their utterances on the law, and they lacked the sophistication

---

6. Anthony Burgess, *Vindiciae legis: or, A vindication of the morall law and the covenants, from the Errours of Papists, Arminians, Socinians, and more especially Antinomians* (London: T. Underhill, 1646), 156–57.

7. Ibid., 157.

8. Henry Burton, *The law and the gospell reconciled* (London, 1631), 3.

9. Ibid.

10. Ibid.

11. Como, *Blown by the Spirit*, 213.

12. Ibid.

found in the writings of men like Sibbes, Goodwin, and Owen. In fact, Ernest Kevan castigates the antinomian Robert Towne for speaking with "two voices" and notes how "exasperating" his arguments are.[13] So when pressed on the issue, many antinomian theologians did not utterly reject any use of the moral law. But the accent in their preaching and writing was decidedly negative when speaking about the law's role in the life of the believer. As Bozeman observes, "If they did not reject outright law's claim to rule the saints, they did largely ignore it."[14] Como likewise suggests that what "was important was not so much what Eaton, Towne and other imputative antinomians said, but what they left unsaid, or rather, what they communicated through subtle and implicit cues and hints."[15]

If believers keep the law, the antinomians said, it is simply because they are so enamored with their free justification. In their view, a true apprehension of free justification causes believers to do good works without any coercion from the law itself. So, in the words of John Eaton (1574/5–1630/31), believers who truly understand their free justification will walk in the steps of Abraham, "whereby like Abraham without the Law of the ten Commandments, we walk holily, soberly, and righteously in all God's Commandments declaratively to man-ward, being zealous of good works."[16] Eaton does not deny that Christians will live "righteously," but he goes against the orthodox when he claims that the commandments are unnecessary for holy living. Moreover, Eaton, like many of his antinomian contemporaries, speaks of keeping the law only in reference to mankind, not to God. Law keeping for the antinomians has a horizontal focus, and not also a vertical focus in terms of our duty toward God. The notion that "God does not need your good works, but your neighbor does" was taken in an absolute sense by the antinomians, who typically missed the obvious Christological point about Christ's ever-increasing glorification as the God-man.[17] In the end, Como's analysis of the antinomians is correct when

---

13. Ernest Kevan, *The Grace of Law: A Study in Puritan Theology* (Grand Rapids: Soli Deo Gloria Publications, 2003), 168.

14. Theodore Dwight Bozeman, *The Precisianist Strain: Disciplinary Religion and Antinomian Backlash in Puritanism to 1638* (Chapel Hill: University of North Carolina Press, 2004), 205.

15. Como, *Blown by the Spirit*, 218.

16. John Eaton, *The discovery of the most dangerous dead faith* (London, 1642), 191–92. Bozeman comments: "Eaton proposed that the experience of justification imparts an ethical sense and will that is simply irrepressible and almost wholly reliable." *The Precisianist Strain*, 193.

17. I will deal more with this phrase in later chapters.

he suggests that "despite their occasional suggestions that believers were to continue to make use of the Law, their deeply negative portrayal of the Decalogue . . . in fact invited listeners to reject the Commandments more decisively."[18] Thus, the use of the written law in sanctification was typically rejected by antinomian theologians, and their own rhetoric concerning the law was typically negative.

LAW AS LAW

What role, if any, does the law play in sanctification? Again, this question needs to be clarified. It does little good to claim, as many antinomians did, that the law does not give "ability" to perform the commands. This misses the point of the debate, for no one would have said that the law acted as "the wind behind the sails." At stake is the question of how precisely the law does or does not aid the sanctification of the believer. The differences between the antinomians and the orthodox on this question are addressed in the minutes of Session 699 of the Westminster Assembly:

> Resolved upon the Q.: 'neither is it an evidence that a man is under the law and not under grace, when he refrains from evil and does good, because the law encourages to the one and deters from the other.'

> Resolved upon the Q.: 'but rather a signe of the power of God's grace in him, when the heart is subdued conscientiously to live according to the rule, though in things contrary to the dictate of corrupt nature, from the consideration of God's goodness in rewarding freely those that do well, and of his justice in punishing them that do ill.'[19]

These words are clearly behind WCF 19.6, where it is said: "So as, a man's doing good, and refraining from evil, because the law encourageth to the one, and deterreth from the other, is no evidence of his being under the law; and not under grace."[20]

18. Como, *Blown by the Spirit*, 218.
19. Chad B. van Dixhoorn, *The Minutes and Papers of the Westminster Assembly, 1643–1652* (Oxford: Oxford University Press, 2012), 4:260.
20. Note also WLC 97: "Although they that are regenerate, and believe in Christ, be delivered from the moral law as a covenant of works, so as thereby they are neither justified nor condemned;

Most antinomians were of the view that Christians obey the law out of gratitude for all that the triune God has done for them. But Reformed theologians, while agreeing that gratitude is a motive for obedience, insisted on the necessity of law keeping because of the Creator-creature distinction (WCF 19.5). Not only can man not escape the obligation to keep God's law, but man's decision to keep God's law because it is God's law is in fact a sign of grace, not a sign of being unconverted or having a legalistic spirit, as the antinomians argued. Attached to God's law are threatenings and promises, which are legitimate reasons why a Christian should keep the moral law. As Rutherford notes, the antinomian schema means the "believer can neither break the Law in order to punishment, nor keep and doe the Law in order to reward . . . because they are freed from all binding and obliging Law."[21] Ezekiel Hopkins (1634–90) argues strongly against the antinomians, who are to be "abominated" because their theology denies the value of God's law by their insistence "that no other obligation to duty lies upon them who are in Christ Jesus, but only from the law of gratitude: that God requires not obedience from them, upon so low and sordid an account, as the fear of his wrath and dread severity; but all is to flow only from the principle of love, and the sweet temper of a grateful and ingenuous spirit."[22] Rutherford sums up the issue well by claiming that the antinomians "make all duties a matter of courtesy."[23]

HEIGHTENED OBLIGATION

Following from the point above about keeping the law as law, Reformed theologians not infrequently spoke of the heightened obligation in the new covenant for Christians to keep God's moral law. As WCF 19.5 makes clear, the moral law perpetually binds even those who have been justified, "not only in regard of the matter contained in it, but also in respect of the

---

yet, besides the general uses thereof common to them with all men, it is of special use, to shew them how much they are bound to Christ for his fulfilling it, and enduring the curse thereof in their stead, and for their good; and thereby to provoke them to more thankfulness, and to express the same in their greater care to conform themselves thereunto as the rule of their obedience."

21. Samuel Rutherford, *A survey of the spirituall antichrist* (London, 1647), 2.97.
22. Ezekiel Hopkins, "An Exposition on the Commandments," in *The Works of Ezekiel Hopkins* (London: L. B. Seeley, 1809), 1:282.
23. Rutherford, *Spirituall antichrist*, 2:29.

authority of God the Creator, who gave it. *Neither doth Christ, in the Gospel, any way dissolve, but much strengthen this obligation*" (emphasis added). That last sentence is crucial and helps us to make sense of the nature of the moral law and holiness in the New Testament.[24] As Goodwin notes, "If God in former ages did reveal himself but by piecemeal, and if that piecemeal knowledge, which they had by inch and inch, did make them holy; for how holy was Enoch and Abraham that had but one promise; then how much more holy should we be, that have had so full a discovery! If one promise wrought so much on their hearts, how much more should so many promises on ours!"[25]

Because of the greater indicatives of the new covenant, the imperatives are not relaxed, but in fact are strengthened. There are a number of examples in the New Testament that confirm this truth, but John 13:34 seems to be the best and clearest example. Jesus speaks of the "new commandment" to love one another in the same way as he has loved them. Readers who are familiar with the Old Testament might find Jesus' words a little perplexing, because the so-called "new" commandment seems to be identical to several Old Testament laws, not to mention the fact that the second table of the law is summed up as "You shall love your neighbor as yourself" (Mark 12:31). Indeed, Leviticus 19:33–34 and Deuteronomy 15:12–18 seem to be commanding the Israelites to love one another as God has loved them. However, the command in the Old Testament to love "as I have loved you" has specific reference to the exodus of God's people out of Egypt. God's gracious dealings with his "treasured possession" (the indicative) provides the reason why they in turn should show the same type of graciousness (the imperative). Christ's words, "as I have loved you" (John 13:34), are directly connected to his own act of humiliation in John 13 (foot washing) and his sacrificial death on the cross (Phil. 2:5–11). Christ's humiliation and sacrifice point to a new way in which believers are to love one another. And this model of love is a greater model of love than what is found in the Old Testament, since it was ontologically impossible for God to act in sacrificial love toward his people. In other words, it was the incarnation that made a suffering love possible, and

24. The following chapter will address the relation between the law and the gospel.
25. Thomas Goodwin, *The Works of Thomas Goodwin, D.D.* (1861–66; repr., Grand Rapids: Reformation Heritage Books, 2006), 5:530.

therefore it was only after the incarnation that this heightened form of love could be required on the basis of Christ's own example. Therefore, contrary to antinomianism, the New Testament heightens, not lessens, the place of the moral law in the life of the believer, for the indicative has been heightened through Christ's mediatorial work.

The command, then, to love one another as Christ has loved us involves a particular application, which necessarily means that our love for others must be sacrificial if it is to reflect Christ's love for us. More than that, while Christians are free from the Mosaic administration, understood in terms of its covenantal significance, they are not free from the unchanging core found in the Decalogue. In various places, Paul's written commands to believers are given in the same form in which they were initially given by Moses to the Israelites. Galatians 5:14 speaks of fulfilling "the whole law" when you love your neighbor as yourself. But while Paul gives a general application of the law in Galatians 5:14, he also is not afraid to give a specific application of the law, in its Decalogue form, in other places, such as Romans 13:8–10 and Ephesians 6:2–3.

This point is absolutely fundamental to the debate. Not infrequently will one hear that we should just "preach the gospel" and then let the Spirit do his work in believers. Of course, this statement can be taken in a number of ways that even the staunchest opponent of antinomianism could agree to. But often there is such an overreaction to "moralizing sermons" that preachers fail to give appropriate, soul-searching application in the form of commands. Direct and specific application is something that Paul does not omit in his letters. For example, he reminds the Thessalonians to love one another and then urges them "to do this more and more" (1 Thess. 4:10). Try harder? Yes. Do more? Yes. For Paul, the law functioned as a means of sanctification. But the antinomians utterly rejected the view that the law could function as an instrument of sanctification.

Saltmarsh affirms that the "Law is now in the Spirit," so that the outward (i.e., written) commandment of the law is unnecessary for new covenant believers who have the law of the Spirit within them.[26] Referring to Saltmarsh's argument, Rutherford states that believers need the direction of the written law. The written law and the law of the Spirit are not

---

26. John Saltmarsh, *Free Grace* (London, 1645), 146.

contrary principles in the life of the believer.[27] Burgess also disputes the notion that the law is not an instrument of sanctification: "If the Law, and the commands thereof be impossible, to what purpose then does he command them? Why does he bid us turn to him when we cannot? Then we answer, that these commandments are not only informing of a duty, but they are practical and operative means appointed by God, to work, at least in some degree, that which is commanded."[28] Burgess is careful, however, to point out that the law will have an effect in sanctification only if it is accompanied by the power of the Spirit. If the Spirit does not accompany the preaching of the law, it will completely fail to sanctify. But this is also true of the gospel: "Preach the promises of the Gospel a thousand times over, they convey no grace, if the Spirit of God be not there effectually."[29] In short, the point that Burgess is zealous to make is simple, namely, that God has appointed means to accomplish his ends. When Paul urges the Thessalonians to do "more and more," he fully expects that God will accompany that command with his Spirit, so that they can in fact show more and more love to one another. We have been constituted in such a way that we need to be given specific commands by ministers of God's Word. To leave off the preaching of commands, as many do today, is to neglect an instrument that God has appointed for the sanctification of his church. We must not be wiser than God!

"THEIR PRINCIPLES"

Of all the claims that are made about antinomian theology, perhaps the least controversial one is that they gave priority to justification over other saving benefits, especially sanctification. A great deal of ink has been spilled by scholars in recent years on precisely this question, and that debate is certainly important. But the debate is far too complex to delve into in any detail. The problem in the seventeenth century among antinomian

27. Rutherford, *Spirituall antichrist*, 2:117–18.
28. Burgess, *Vindiciae legis*, 188.
29. Ibid., 189. See also Rutherford's similar comments in opposition to the antinomian view that the law is not an instrument of sanctification: "But compare the Law and the Gospel both in their Letter: . . . It's true, the Gospel promises a new heart and grace, and righteousness to the elect, which the Law as Law doth not. But the Gospel in its letter doth no more give grace and righteousness than the Law. . . . That which we are commanded to do by the grace of Christ, as a testimony of our thankfulness . . . and to be a rule of life, obliging us so to walk, that is a means of our sanctification." *Spirituall antichrist*, 2:236–37.

theologians was the *degree* to which they gave justification a priority in their theology. As noted above, the antinomians essentially subsumed sanctification under justification.[30] The gospel was, in their view, synonymous with justification.[31] The degree to which they prioritized justification over other graces was, in short, totally unhelpful, and their interpretation of various passages in Scripture inevitably suffered from such an approach. Thomas Goodwin highlights this very problem. Commenting on Philippians 1:10 ("so that you may approve what is excellent, and so be pure and blameless for the day of Christ"), he asserts that, in explaining how Paul's prayer will be answered, "an antinomian would be ready to give an easy answer with respect to their principles: that all is accomplished in justification."[32] But, as Goodwin correctly argues, the blamelessness spoken of in Philippians 1:10 "is not that of justification, but sanctification."[33]

When "their principles" are used, passages are misinterpreted. A number of texts come to mind that can easily be distorted with this type of hermeneutic. For example, when Christ says, "For I tell you, unless your righteousness exceeds that of the scribes and Pharisees, you will never enter the kingdom of heaven" (Matt. 5:20), he was not speaking of his own imputed righteousness. After all, according to the Scriptures, the Pharisees did not actually keep God's law; they "leave the commandment of God and hold to the tradition of men" (Mark 7:8). Those described in Romans 8:4 surpass the scribes and Pharisees in righteousness (cf. Matt. 5:6; Ps. 106:3) because their obedience is wrought by the Spirit, and far more precise and extensive.

Psalms 15 and 24 present us with a different type of example. In Psalm 24:3–4, the psalmist asks:

> Who shall ascend the hill of the LORD?
> And who shall stand in his holy place?

---

30. See also Rutherford, *Spirituall antichrist*, 2:46.

31. See, for example, John Eaton, *The honey-combe of free justification by Christ alone* (London, 1642), especially "The Preface to the Reader." He claims that people are only truly born again when "for the assurance of their salvation, they wholly rest in the joyful knowledge & full sufficiency of their free Justification" (7). "Yea let us know for a certainty, that free justification is the very head, heart, and soul of all Christian religion, and true worship of God." "All the righteousness of our unperfect Sanctification is (as the Prophet says) as filthy, monstrous, stained rags, Isa. 64:6" (7–8). "It is of all the rest of the benefits of the Gospel, which all depend upon this benefit" (9).

32. Goodwin, *Works*, 7:153.

33. Ibid.

> He who has clean hands and a pure heart,
>> who does not lift up his soul to what is false
>> and does not swear deceitfully.

Just as it would be wrong to suggest that this psalm is true only of God's people, and not preeminently of God's Son, so it would be incorrect to suggest that it is true only of Jesus and nobody else. The only reason this psalm can be referred to God's people is because of Christ's pure heart and his perfect and perpetual obedience on their behalf. We are allowed to enter, first, because we have been clothed with the imputed righteousness of Christ and thus are accepted in God's sight. But when we read passages such as this in light of our union with Christ, rather than with the idea that the doctrine of justification is the only or governing hermeneutical principle, we are surely not incorrect to understand this psalm as a call to worship for those who are not only accepted but also renewed in Christ. Ministers should use this psalm to exhort their people that if they want to worship God, they must do so with "clean hands and a pure heart" (see also 1 Tim. 1:5; James 4:8). After all, in the Beatitudes, Jesus blesses "the pure in heart" and promises that they will see God (Matt. 5:8). John Calvin's comments on these verses are noteworthy: "But David here treats of those who may lawfully enter into God's sanctuary."[34] Similar comments could be made on other passages of Scripture, such as Psalm 1, where the righteous are the true Israelites whose "delight is in the law of the LORD" (v. 2). But when justification becomes the central dogma of our biblical interpretation, Psalm 1 becomes mere wishful thinking (or not even that!).

CONCLUSION

This chapter has been focused on the different views of the law held by the antinomians and the orthodox Reformed theologians in Puritan England. The issues discussed above are just some of the areas of disagreement, but, I hope, they clarify the nature of the debate. So is the law, accompanied by the Spirit, a true means of our sanctification? Yes

34. John Calvin, *Commentary on the Book of Psalms*, trans. James Anderson (1846; repr., Grand Rapids: Baker, 1979), 1:404. Calvin comments on Psalm 15 that David is speaking of believers. In fact, if there is a criticism of Calvin on this point, it is that he is not sufficiently Christocentric in his exposition of these psalms.

(Rom. 7:12). Moreover, even the preaching of the gospel requires the power of the Holy Spirit, for apart from the Spirit's work, the gospel cannot convert sinners or sanctify saints. But our discussion of the law is not over. In the next chapter, the relationship between the law and the gospel will be analyzed, thus answering several questions that were left unanswered in this chapter.

What I hope has been made clear, however, is the fact that though we are justified, we are not therefore completely wise and inherently holy through and through. Christians need specific moral exhortations because our hearts have the remnant of sin and we have darkened minds. The writer to the Hebrews clearly grasped this; there would be little point to exhort one another continually, so "that none of you may be hardened by the deceitfulness of sin" (Heb. 3:13), if "gospelizing" will take care of everything. Moreover, Paul is quite specific in telling Timothy to charge the rich with particular duties (1 Tim. 6:17–19). The tendencies of the rich to commit certain sins require specific exhortations to avoid them. Of course, when faced with this passage, few will deny the plain teaching of Scripture. But, as I have noted already, the problem is not always the "rational" antinomianism of preachers and teachers, but their "practical" antinomianism, whereby they essentially fail to bring home such exhortations to their listeners who need them. And Christians do need to hear exhortations concerning God's moral requirements of them, for "great peace have those who love your law" (Ps. 119:165).

4

THE LAW AND THE GOSPEL

"THAT THE GOSPEL HAS THE FORCE OF A
LAW, I SHALL EVIDENCE BY THESE CONSID-
ERATIONS." —THOMAS MANTON[1]

DEBATES BETWEEN the orthodox Reformed and the antinomians involved several interrelated points of divinity. Because in theology all doctrines are related to one another, the errors of the antinomians were not limited to the role of the law in the life of the believer. In his well-known attack on antinomianism, Samuel Rutherford notes that the relation between the law and the gospel is central to the controversy with the antinomians.[2] Gert van den Brink says that the antinomians "saw an absolute contrast between Law and Gospel."[3] He cites Thomas Shepard, who argues that the "fundamental error of the Antinomians" centered on their insistence that the "law requires doing, but the gospel no doing."[4] Shepard also states that while the gospel requires "no doing" in the matter of justification, it nevertheless commands God's people to be holy and perfect.[5] Shepard's view was fairly commonplace among Reformed theologians, particularly in

1. Thomas Manton, *The Complete Works of Thomas Manton* (London: J. Nisbet, 1870–75), 11:398.
2. Samuel Rutherford, *A survey of the spirituall antichrist* (London, 1647), 2:120.
3. G. A. van den Brink, "Calvin, Witsius (1636–1708) and the English Antinomians," in *The Reception of John Calvin and His Theology in Reformed Orthodoxy*, ed. Andreas J. Beck and William den Boer (Leiden: Brill, 2011), 232.
4. Thomas Shepard, *The Works of Thomas Shepard* (Boston: Doctrinal Tract and Book Society, 1853), 3:92.
5. Ibid.

Puritan England. Precisely what he and others meant by the gospel demanding holiness and perfection will be addressed in some detail below, since that is at the heart of the debate between the orthodox Reformed and the antinomians in Britain and New England during the seventeenth century.

The distinction between the law and the gospel was affirmed by all Reformed theologians. Luther and the Lutherans likewise distinguished between the law and the gospel. In their view, the ability to distinguish properly between law and gospel was essential to being a good Christian theologian. The problem, of course, is not that the distinction is supposedly Lutheran. One would have to excise hundreds of books from the Reformation and post-Reformation eras in order to come to such a conclusion. Rather, the real point of contention in debates on antinomianism—indeed, even in Reformed circles these days—is how the law-gospel distinction is formulated. Even Lutheran theologians have disagreed with one another on the precise details of the distinction.[6] Likewise, Reformed versions of the law-gospel distinction have raised not a few eyebrows (and scorn) from Lutheran theologians for reasons that will be considered in this chapter.

"UTTERLY INCONSISTENT"

If there was any question on which Reformed, Lutheran, and antinomian theologians agreed, it was on whether works were required for justification. With one voice, they deplored such an idea. Owen, for example, affirms this principle: "It is true, our works and grace are opposed in the matter of justification, as utterly inconsistent; if it be of works it is not of grace, and if it be of grace it is not of works."[7] Burgess focuses on how important the doctrine of justification is for a believer, because once the Protestant doctrine of justification is given up, man is necessarily brought into himself. To prevent us from depending upon ourselves, God declares us righteous apart from works (Rom. 4:6). Burgess approvingly cites Luther's famous statement: "Take heed, not only of thy sins, but also of thy good

6. See Timothy J. Wengert, *Law and Gospel: Philip Melanchthon's Debate with John Agricola of Eisleben over* Poenitentia (Grand Rapids: Baker Books, 1997), 177ff. Wengert's chapter on Melanchthon's development of the third use of the law is particularly stimulating.

7. John Owen, *The Works of John Owen, D.D.*, ed. William H. Goold (Edinburgh: Johnstone & Hunter, 1850–55), 3:384.

duties."[8] Immediately thereafter, Burgess notes that if this were all that the antinomians argued for, then "none would contradict it"—but they take this precious truth and draw many unsound conclusions from it.[9]

The role of works in relation to justification is vastly different from its role in relation to sanctification. Richard Sibbes sets forth the issue in his usual evocative manner: "I say there are two courts: one of justification, another of sanctification. In the court of justification merits are nothing worth, insufficient; but in the court of sanctification, as they are ensigns of a sanctified course, so they are jewels and ornaments."[10] More recently, John Murray has stated that "the simple truth is that if law is conceived of as contributing in the least degree towards our acceptance with God and our justification by him, then the gospel of grace is a nullity."[11] However, with this salient truth established, the relation between law and grace or the relation between the law and the gospel is not purely one of antithesis. Here is precisely where the battle lines begin to be drawn in the debate and differences emerge among Reformed, Lutheran, and antinomian theologians.[12]

INDICATIVE ONLY?

What is the gospel? This question has been debated since the time of Christ. It was vigorously debated in Puritan England, and today scholars and theologians are continually crossing swords on this much-vexed topic. The main area of concern, *in its crassest form*, seems to be the idea that the

8. Anthony Burgess, *Vindiciae legis: or, A vindication of the morall law and the covenants, from the Errours of Papists, Arminians, Socinians, and more especially Antinomians* (London: T. Underhill, 1646), 23.

9. Ibid. See also his comments on Romans 3:27 in ibid., 228–29.

10. Richard Sibbes, *The Complete Works of Richard Sibbes* (Edinburgh: James Nichol, 1862–64), 5:85.

11. John Murray, *Principles of Conduct: Aspects of Biblical Ethics* (Grand Rapids: Eerdmans, 1957), 182.

12. Readers should consult the exchange between Michael Horton and Mark A. Garcia, "I. Law and Gospel," in *The Confessional Presbyterian Journal* 8 (2012): 154–76. Michael Horton does a fine job of showing how Protestants have historically held to an absolute contrast between the law and the gospel in the matter of justification. But his article does not venture into the territory that is in dispute. As Garcia notes in his response, the law-gospel distinction in the matter of justification "is straightforward and needs no defense, and given how tirelessly Horton has tried to demonstrate the point I regret that our agreement on this renders the bulk of Horton's presentation moot" (172). At issue is the way in which some use the law-gospel distinction as a hermeneutic, and how Lutheran and Reformed theologians have differed on this distinction. The earlier discussion in this chapter addresses issues that I had hoped Horton would speak to in his article.

gospel is essentially synonymous with the doctrine of justification. Thus, if the gospel is roughly synonymous with justification, then it has nothing to do with what happens "in" believers, but only with what happens "for" believers. In other words, does the gospel pertain only to Christ's works of impetation, or is his work of application also part of the gospel? Simply distinguishing between the indicative and the imperative does not answer the question, for the work of Christ in the believer is also an indicative (i.e., his work). The law-gospel issue helps to answer these questions.

Antinomian theologians were, at best, vague on this particular issue. Yet Van den Brink's assessment, quoted above, seems accurate, namely, that for the antinomians there was an absolute contrast between the law and the gospel. Saltmarsh defines the gospel as "Christ himself" or the "glad tidings of what he hath done and suffered for sinners."[13] Commenting on this issue, Bozeman cites the antinomian Roger Brierley (1586–1637) and contends that his view was shared by Eaton and the other antinomians, that is, "'The whole Doctrine of the Gospel, is not what we should do to [serve] God, but what we should receive from him.'"[14] The problem was not, of course, with what was said. Who could find fault with defining the gospel as "Christ himself"? But as is so often the case in theological debates on antinomianism, what the antinomians did not say proved to be what many Reformed theologians took issue with. Burgess and other Reformed divines in the post-Reformation era were scholastic theologians, and therefore constantly made use of distinctions in order to set forth their respective views more clearly. The question of defining the gospel was no different. Burgess argued that just as the law may be understood "largely" and "strictly," so too can the word "gospel." He writes, "In the Scripture it is sometimes taken more largely, and sometimes more strictly: when it's taken largely, it signifies the whole doctrine that the Apostles were to preach . . . the doctrine and preaching of Christ. Or else it is taken most strictly, as when Luke 2.10. Behold, I bring you glad tidings . . . in which strict sense it's called the Gospel of peace."[15] With this distinction in mind, similar distinctions between the forensic and the renovative, or impetration and application, or redemptive-historical and existential, or transient and

13. John Saltmarsh, *Free Grace* (London, 1645), 138.
14. Theodore Dwight Bozeman, *The Precisianist Strain: Disciplinary Religion and Antinomian Backlash in Puritanism to 1638* (Chapel Hill: University of North Carolina Press, 2004), 200.
15. Burgess, *Vindiciae legis*, 230–31.

applicatory, can be understood in relation to the gospel narrowly and broadly conceived. The gospel can be considered as a pure indicative only when taken strictly; taken largely (the more typical way of speaking), it involves both the indicative and the imperative. The Puritans, such as Rutherford, Owen, and Manton, typically referred to the gospel in its broad sense, which will be the focus of this chapter.

GOSPEL THREATENINGS

Both Reformed and antinomian theologians affirmed that the law threatens and that the gospel promises (Gal. 3:10–14). But the law also promises life (Lev. 18:5; Deut. 4:1; Ezek. 20:21; Rom. 10:5), though precisely what this means has been the subject of much dispute. For the purposes of this chapter, the question that must be raised is whether the gospel not only promises, but also threatens. And if the gospel threatens, does it threaten only unbelievers or also believers? The Canons of Dort shed some light on this question, but a great deal of analysis is required in order to determine the intention of the document. Relevant to the present question is the Fifth Head of Doctrine ("Of the Perseverance of the Saints"), article 14. Most English versions read: "And as it hath pleased God, by the preaching of the gospel, to begin this work of grace in us, so he preserves, continues, and perfects it by the hearing and reading of his Word, by meditation thereon, and by the exhortations, threatenings, and promises thereof, as well as by the use of the sacraments." Those who deny that the gospel threatens may argue that the "threatenings" here refer to God's Word, which contains both threatenings and promises, that is, "law" and "gospel." However, this line of reasoning does not appear to do justice to the authorized translations. The Latin, Dutch, and French versions of the Canons of Dort are the authorized versions, not the English. These versions (and their English translations) read as follows:

> Latin: "Quemadmodum autem Deo placuit, opus hoc suum gratiæ per prædicationem Euangelij in nobis inchoare, ita per eiusdem auditum, lectionem, meditationem, adhortationes, minas, promissa, nec non per usum Sacrementorum illud censeruat, continuat, & perficit."[16]

16. *Acta Synodi Nationalis: in nomine Domini nostri Jesu Christi* (Dordrechti: Isaaci Joannidis Canini, 1620), 41–42.

English Translation: "As it has pleased God to begin his work of grace in us by the preaching of the gospel, so he preserves, continues and perfects it through the hearing, reading, meditation, exhortations, threatenings, [and] promises of that same gospel, and also through the use of the sacraments."

Dutch: "Gelijk het God nu beliefd heeft dit Zijn werk der genade door de predikatie des Evangelies in ons te beginnen, alzoo bewaart, achtervolgt en volbrengt Hij hetzelve door het hooren, lezen en overleggen er van, mitsgaders, vermaningen, dreigementen, beloften en het gebruik der H. Sacramenten."[17]

English Translation: "Just as it now has pleased God to begin in us this work of grace by the preaching of the gospel, so also he preserves, continues, and brings it to fullness by the hearing, reading, and meditation thereof, also through exhortations, threats, promises, and the use of the holy sacraments."

French: "Et comme il a pleu à Dieu commencer en nous par sa grace, ce sien oeuvre par la predication de l'Euangile: de mesme il le conferee, continne, & l'accomplit par l'ouye, la lecture, meditation, exhortation, menasses & promesses du mesme Evangile, comme aussi par l'usage des Sacremens."[18]

English Translation: "And as it has pleased God [*lit.*, given pleasure to God] to begin in us by his grace, this his work by the preaching of the gospel: just so he confirms it, maintains and fulfills it by the hearing,

---

17. *Acta of Handelingen der Nationale Synode, in den naam onzes Heeren Jezus Christus, gehouden door autoriteit der Hoogmogende Heeren Staten-Generaal der Vereenigde Nederlanden te Dordrecht, ten jare 1618 en 1619*, ed. J. H. Donner and S. A. van den Hoorn (Leiden: D. Donner, 1883–86), 278. In this same document (429) you find this statement from the Palatinate (Pfalz) theologians: "Beide werkt de H. Geest door het Evangelie, wanneer Hij met bevelen ons port, met beloften aanlokt en met dreigementen verschrikt" ("The Holy Spirit works through the gospel when he both prods us with commands, draws us with promises, and terrifies us with threats"). The Swiss theologians (491) speak of "Evangelische bevelen, aanradende vermaningen, groote beloften der hoogste goederen, of daartegenover, door afmaningen en dreigementen" ("Gospel commands, exhortations, admonitions, great promises of the highest goods, or, on the other hand, through deterrents and threats").

18. *Jugement du Synode National des Eglises Reformees du Pays-Bas, tenu à Dordrecht l'An 1618 et 1619* (Nismes: Jean Vaguenar, 1620), 53.

reading, meditation, exhortation, threats and promises of the same gospel, as also by the use of the sacraments."

The official French translation (1620) cited above is explicit that the threats come by "the same gospel" ("du mesme Evangile"). The Dutch version is perhaps a little more ambiguous than the French, but the same conclusion should be reached, namely, that both the promises and the threatenings come from the gospel. The Latin version is decisive. The phrase "hearing, reading, meditation, exhortations, threatenings, [and] promises" is modified by "eiusdem," a genitive pronoun meaning "the same," which can only refer back to "Euangelii," meaning "the gospel." Thus, the "threatenings" belong to "that same gospel" which is preached. So the gospel, according to the Canons of Dort, contains threatenings as well as promises.

In England, John Owen addressed the topic of "gospel threatenings" in his exposition of Hebrews. He identifies three categories of people who are the objects of gospel threatenings: unbelievers, spurious believers, and true believers.[19] Owen adduces numerous passages in the New Testament that speak to the first category of persons (e.g., John 3:36; Rom. 2:8–9; 2 Thess. 1:6–10; 1 Peter 4:17–18). He affirms that these passages are "evangelical, inasmuch as they are proper to the gospel, and distinct from all the threatenings of the law."[20] There are also those who belong to the church of Jesus Christ, but are not genuine believers. They are those whom Christ warns with strong language and examples (e.g., Heb. 12:15–17).[21] The third category refers to those who are true believers and yet receive gospel threatenings. They receive warnings, for example, in the letters to the seven churches in the book of Revelation (see Rev. 3:14–22). Owen argues that gospel threatenings aimed at believers are "suited unto their good and advantage . . . for believers are subject to sloth and security, to wax dead, dull, cold, and formal in their course. . . . To awake them, warn them, and excite them unto a renewal of their obedience, does God set before them the threatenings mentioned. See Rev. 2–3."[22] Not only the letters to the seven churches, but also passages in Paul's epistles, prove this point. For instance, Paul warns believers that "if you live according to the flesh you

19. Owen, *Works*, 21:206.
20. Ibid., 21:206.
21. Ibid., 21:207–8.
22. Ibid., 21:209.

will die, but if by the Spirit you put to death the deeds of the body, you will live" (Rom. 8:13). This is not a "law threatening," but rather a "gospel threatening." In the WCF, believers are those who yield obedience to God's commands, tremble at his threatenings, and embrace his promises (14.2). God's commands, threatenings, and promises for believers are all derived from the gospel, largely understood. In fact, the most severe warnings in the Scriptures are made to professing Christians, and for that reason they are gospel warnings (see Heb. 10:26–31).

Antinomians, past and present, do not hold to the view that the gospel threatens. But how many preachers today hold to a view of the gospel that accords with what one finds in the Canons of Dort? Often, any "threatening" is understood as a "law threatening," and so the "gospel" is held out to believers as a means of escaping such a threatening. The threatening, then, loses its force and necessary application. But, as Owen notes, gospel threatenings are for the good of believers, in order that they may persevere to the end in renewed obedience to the one who is both lawgiver and rewarder.[23]

A PRESCRIPTIVE AND GRACIOUS GOSPEL

Rutherford's work against the antinomians deals with dozens of inter-related points of contention. He shows himself to be particularly zealous when it comes to defining the gospel. In his view, the gospel is not simply an account of what God has done in Christ Jesus. It certainly is that, but the gospel also contains imperatives. Rutherford notes the position of Robert Towne, who claims that *"The Gospel . . . persuades rather than commands."*[24] However, speaking for the orthodox, Rutherford writes: "But say we, it both commands, (as the Law does) and with a more strong obligation of the constraining love of Christ . . . so here be no differences at all."[25] Was Rutherford's view that the gospel "commands" echoed by anyone else in the Reformed tradition?[26] Or has Rutherford slipped into a form of neono-

---

23. The list of Reformed theologians who affirm a gospel that commands, threatens, and promises is large. Whether their supposed conflation of law and gospel owes to a Barthian influence is something worth considering, but I suspect such a study might not get very far!

24. Rutherford, *Spirituall antichrist*, 2:122.

25. Ibid.

26. On John Calvin's position, see Van den Brink, "Calvin, Witsius (1636–1708) and the English Antinomians," 238–39.

mianism and thus compromised the gracious nature of a gospel that says "done" whereas the law says "do"?

In agreement with Rutherford, Owen holds that the gospel "commands" believers in the matter of holiness: "My meaning is, that the word, the gospel, the doctrine of Christ, in the preceptive part of it, is so the rule of all our obedience and holiness as that all which it requires belongs thereunto, and nothing else but what it requires does so; and the formal reason of our holiness consists in conformity thereunto, under this consideration, that it is the word and doctrine of Christ."[27] Nothing can be considered holiness except what the gospel requires. Owen cites Titus 2:11–12[28] and Ephesians 4:22–24[29] as passages exemplifying the "preceptive part of the gospel."[30] Paul's letter to the Ephesians is a gospel letter, which includes both indicatives (chapters 1–3) and imperatives (chapters 4–6).[31]

Thomas Shepard also adopts this position. He polemicizes against the antinomians, who, as noted above, claim that under the gospel there is "no doing." He affirms that "as the gospel exacts no doing, that thereby we may be just, so it requires doing also when by Christ Jesus we are made just."[32] More specifically, the gospel requires believers to be holy and perfect because God is holy and perfect. In fact, he contends that the law and the gospel each require as much perfection as the other in the matter of holiness. But there is a crucial difference ("which many have not observed"), namely, that the gospel does not require this perfection in the same way as the law. For "the law calling and urging of it that so hereby we may be made just, it therefore accepts of nothing but perfection; but the gospel requiring it because we are perfectly just already in Christ, hence, though it commands us as much as the law, yet it accepts of less, even the least measure of sincerity and perfection mixed with the greatest measure of imperfection."[33] Shepard's

27. Owen, *Works*, 3:507–8.
28. "For the grace of God has appeared, bringing salvation for all people, training us to renounce ungodliness and worldly passions, and to live self-controlled, upright, and godly lives in the present age."
29. You have been taught "to put off your old self, which belongs to your former manner of life and is corrupt through deceitful desires, and to be renewed in the spirit of your minds, and to put on the new self, created after the likeness of God in true righteousness and holiness."
30. Owen, *Works*, 3:605.
31. Of course, even when Paul moves to the imperatives, he cannot help but return again and again to the indicatives (e.g., 2 Cor. 5:14–15).
32. Shepard, *Works*, 3:92.
33. Ibid. For a fuller defense of this position, see Owen, *Works*, 3:606–9.

comments are extremely helpful for a number of reasons. He notes that the law and the gospel both require perfection. However, the law requires absolute perfection for anyone to be justified, whereas in the gospel those who are freely justified (WCF 11.1) may serve God with sincere, albeit imperfect, obedience (WCF 16.6). Since we are accepted in Christ, our worship and obedience is acceptable to God (1 Peter 2:5).

This explains why, in Genesis 26:5, Abraham can be described as having kept God's commandments, statutes, and laws, even though by that time Abraham had broken the ninth commandment (on two occasions) by calling Sarah his sister (Gen. 12:13; 20:2). King David, notwithstanding his sordid history involving Bathsheba and Uriah, kept God's commandments and followed him with all of his heart (1 Kings 14:8). Similarly, Noah is described as a righteous and blameless man (Gen. 6:9; see also Job 1:1, 8; Luke 1:6).[34] Because of the gospel, God accepted their sincere obedience, though it was imperfect, whereas the law would have condemned them for those imperfections in spite of their sincerity. This is not the same thing as Baxter's neonomianism, because justification excludes our law keeping even under the gospel. In accepting gospel obedience in the context of sanctification, God often refers to his saints as blameless and righteous, which is an exquisite testimony of his graciousness toward his people.

Thomas Manton, with an obvious dig at the antinomians, goes so far as to say, "They err certainly, that tell us the gospel is no law; for if there were no law, there would be no governor . . . no duty, no sin, no judgment, no punishment, nor reward."[35] With this principle in mind, he states in his comments on Psalm 119:34,[36] in the same way as Shepard does above, that keeping the law with the whole heart may be understood legally or evangelically. Taken legally, the rigor of the law "requires exact conformity, without the least motion to the contrary, either in thought or desire, a full obedience to the law with all the powers of the whole man."[37] Man is unable to fulfill the terms of the law in this manner, which is why Christ's perfect law keeping on behalf of his people was necessary. However, in an evangeli-

34. One will find a valuable discussion of the different senses in which a believer may be perfect in Francis Turretin, *Institutes of Elenctic Theology*, ed. James T. Dennison Jr., trans. George Musgrave Giger (Phillipsburg, NJ: P&R Publishing, 1992), 17.2.4.
35. Manton, *Works*, 11:395.
36. "Give me understanding, that I may keep your law and observe it with my whole heart."
37. Manton, *Works*, 6:356.

cal sense, "according to the moderation of the second covenant," God, "out of his love and mercy in Christ Jesus, accepts of such a measure of love and obedience as answers to the measure of sanctification received."[38] Likewise, Ezekiel Hopkins comments: "That God accepts of our obedience, if it be *sinceré voto et conamine*, 'in earnest desires and endeavours.' Although we cannot attain that perfect exactness and spotless purity, which the Law requires: yet we are accepted through Christ, according to what we have, and not according to what we have not."[39]

By showing that God accepts imperfect, but sincere, obedience from his saints, Manton and Hopkins highlight the graciousness of the covenant of grace. Instead of explaining away Psalm 119:34 as impossible, Manton proves that because of our union with Christ, and all that that means, Christians can actually pray this prayer in hopeful expectation that God, to quote Augustine (354–430) (and Sibbes above), gives what he demands and demands whatever he pleases (Heb. 13:21). In other words, Christians can answer to the legal demands of the law in their justification in and through Christ and also the gospel demands of the law in their sanctification by the Spirit. While the errors of perfectionism have been and always will be a threat to true Christian religion, the opposite error of practical antinomianism, whereby preachers fail to exhort their people to obey God with a pure heart, is equally pernicious because such a view undermines the grace of God in saving sinners from the power of sin. Moreover, antinomians typically fail to make the distinction between what the law requires and what the gospel requires, and only focus on the former. Not surprisingly, then, they are flummoxed by so many passages in the Bible that seem to speak of the saints obeying God's law "with their whole heart."

"SWEETLY COMPLY"

The WCF claims that the moral law does "sweetly comply" with the grace of the gospel (19.7). Owen seems to capture what this means when he discusses how believers must pursue holiness. While not explicitly naming his opponents, there is little doubt that he has in mind the antinomians as

---

38. Ibid., 6:357. Manton, following the KJV, took Psalm 119:34 as a personal promise.

39. Ezekiel Hopkins, *The Works of Ezekiel Hopkins* (London: L. B. Seeley, 1809), 1:283. John Owen writes: "There is grace administered by the promises of the gospel, enabling us to perform the obedience of it in that way and manner which God will accept." *Works*, 3:621.

he speaks of the relationship between God's commands and his promises, that is, between duty and grace. In Owen's mind, "Some would separate these things, as inconsistent. A command they suppose leaves no room for a promise, at least not such a promise as wherein God should take on himself to work in us what the command requires of us; and a promise they think takes off all the influencing authority of the command. 'If holiness be our duty, there is no room for grace in this matter; and if it be an effect of grace, there is no place for duty.' But all these arguings are a fruit of the wisdom of the flesh."[40] Owen is careful to add that works and grace are opposed in justification. However, in the matter of personal holiness, duty and grace are not opposed; in fact, "the one does absolutely suppose the other."[41] He adds: "Neither can we perform our duty herein without the grace of God; nor does God give us this grace unto any other end but that we may rightly perform our duty. He that shall deny either that God commands us to be holy in a way of duty, or promises to work holiness in us in a way of grace, may with as much modesty reject the whole Bible."[42]

Since the gospel is an indicative that has imperatives embedded in it (1 Tim. 1:9–11; 2 Thess. 1:8; Rom. 10:16), the antithesis between the law and the gospel ends the moment someone becomes a Christian. Richard Gaffin explains how the gospel abolishes the aforementioned antithesis: "Briefly, apart from the gospel and outside of Christ the law is my enemy and condemns me. Why? Because God is my enemy and condemns me. But with the gospel and in Christ, united to him by faith, the law is no longer my enemy but my friend. Why? Because now God is no longer my enemy but my friend, and the law, his will, the law in its moral core, as reflective of his character and of concerns eternally inherent in his own person and so of what pleases him, is now my friendly guide for life in fellowship with God."[43] Centuries earlier, Theodore Beza (1519–1605) showed how the preaching of the law "begins to change the effect in us (after our disposition is changed) in such a way that instead of making us afraid, it comforts us (1 John 2:17; 2 Peter 1:11–12); instead of where it showed us our condemnation already prepared, it serves us now as a guide to show

40. Owen, *Works*, 3:384.
41. Ibid.
42. Ibid.
43. Richard B. Gaffin Jr., *"By Faith, Not By Sight": Paul and the Order of Salvation* (Milton Keynes, UK: Paternoster, 2006), 103.

us good works (Jer. 21:33; Rom. 7:22) in which we are prepared to walk (Eph. 2:10). Instead of being an unpleasant and unbearable yoke, now it is agreeable to us, easy and light (Matt. 11:30)."[44] In speaking of the law—that is, the so-called "third use" of it—we who are believers are faced with the inescapable reality, though perhaps frightening to some, that Psalm 119 is something we can sing not only about Christ and to Christ, but also about ourselves because of our union with him—and enjoy doing so!

When the law and the gospel are conceived in this manner, clear differences emerge, not only between Reformed and antinomian theology, but also between Reformed and Lutheran theology. The emphases in each tradition are different, and there is little question that the Reformed have a greater affinity for the third use of the law. Of course, this is not to suggest that the Lutherans have never held to the third use of the law, but they always seem to end up giving priority to its "second use." As Richard Muller notes, "The law, for Lutheranism, can never become the ultimate norm for Christian living but, instead, must always lead to Christ who alone is righteous. This difference between the Lutherans and the Reformed arises out of the dialectical relationship of law and gospel in Lutheranism as opposed to the simple distinction of law and gospel within the one *foedus gratiae* held among the Reformed."[45] On this particular point, the antinomians had much more in common with the Lutherans than they did with the Reformed. So the issue is not so much whether one holds to a threefold use of the law, but which use is primary.[46]

A strong distinction between law (as imperative) and gospel (as indicative) does not fit well with the evidence one finds in the Scriptures. For example, Paul speaks negatively of the law in several places. In Romans, he shows its impotence, apart from the Spirit, to give the life it promises. In Romans 7, the law is placed on the Spirit's side of the

---

44. James T. Dennison Jr., ed., *Reformed Confessions of the 16th and 17th Centuries*, vol. 2, *1552–1566* (Grand Rapids: Reformation Heritage Books, 2010), 281.

45. Richard A. Muller, *Dictionary of Latin and Greek Theological Terms: Drawn Principally from Protestant Scholastic Theology* (Grand Rapids: Baker, 2001), 321. See also Robert Kolb, "Law and Gospel in Early Lutheran Dogmatics," in *The Beauty and the Bands*, ed. John R. Fehrmann, Daniel Preus, and Bruce Lukas (Crestwood, MO: Luther Academy, and Minneapolis: Association of Confessional Lutherans, 1995), 55–56.

46. Of course, there may be theologians in the Reformed tradition who have held to such a position, but the commonplace view is the one described above. Literally hundreds of quotations could be added from Reformed theologians showing their view of a "large" (commanding) gospel, understood also as "the doctrine of Christ's teaching."

Spirit-flesh antithesis. Sin condemns because the law exposes sinners. However, in Romans 8, the law becomes a liberating power because of the Spirit. Mortifying sin "by the Spirit" is indeed good news, because we do not kill sin by our own strength, but by the strength of the Holy Spirit. The promise of life (i.e., reward) to those who mortify their sin is contrasted with the threat of death for those who do not mortify their sin (Rom. 8:12–13). My mortification of sin is "good news" because life is promised. If I do not mortify sin, I die. As Owen said, "You must leave your sins or your God."[47]

Often in Paul's writings, the "law" is not placed on the expected side of the antithesis. In 1 Corinthians 7:19, there is a contrast that runs counter to a strict law-gospel distinction: "For neither circumcision counts for anything nor uncircumcision, but keeping the commandments of God." Similarly, in Romans 3:27, Paul contrasts a "law of works" with a "law of faith." Moreover, in agreement with what has been said above, the law actually becomes a quickening Spirit that sets us free from sin and death. By this principle, the righteous requirement of the law is fulfilled in believers (Rom. 8:1–4). The letter does indeed kill, but the Spirit gives life (2 Cor. 3:6). As Zacharias Ursinus (1534–83) notes so well in his commentary on the Heidelberg Catechism, "The law alone, without the gospel, is the letter [that kills] . . . But when it is joined with the gospel, which is the Spirit, it also commences to become the Spirit, which is effectual in the godly, inasmuch as those who are regenerated commence willingly and cheerfully to yield obedience to the law."[48] Here Ursinus speaks not only of the law being "friendly" to believers, but also of the gospel's relation to the Spirit's work in believers. In fact, he adds, "the gospel is the Spirit; that is, it is the ministration and means through which the Holy Ghost, which works spiritual obedience in us, is given."[49] The gospel, largely understood, involves the work of the Spirit in applying Christ's works of impetration. Thus, the law is changed by the Spirit into something effectual, so that we may accurately claim—as was highlighted in the previous chapter—that the law is an instrument in progressive sanctification.

47. Owen, *Works*, 3:576.
48. Zacharias Ursinus, *The Commentary of Dr. Zacharias Ursinus on the Heidelberg Catechism*, trans. G. W. Williard (Cincinnati: Elm Street Printing Company, 1888), 617.
49. Ibid.

REDEMPTION ACCOMPLISHED AND APPLIED

Given the emphasis above on the gospel largely considered, the distinction affirmed by Burgess should not be forgotten. The gospel, in its narrow sense, points to the person and work of Jesus Christ. Jesus Christ crucified, raised, and ascended is the essence of the gospel message (1 Cor. 15:1–4; Rom. 1:1–4). Christ's accomplished work (i.e., impetration), must always be uppermost as the gospel is presented. But redemption accomplished necessarily involves redemption applied. The order of salvation (*ordo salutis*) requires the history of salvation (*historia salutis*). Christ's atoning, substitutionary sacrifice (Rom. 3:24–25) effects reconciliation (Rom. 5:9; 1 Peter 3:18) between sinners and God. But redemption is not the redemption of a sinner until it is applied.

Another way to understand this distinction is that the order of salvation must first be in Christ before it can be in his people. This point does not collapse the distinction between *historia salutis* and *ordo salutis* (i.e., impetration and application), but it does show that every element in the order of salvation is rooted and grounded in Christ's own person and then applied to those who are in union with him. Christ was called (Heb. 10:5–7), justified (1 Tim. 3:16), adopted (Ps. 2:7; Rom. 1:4), sanctified (Rom. 6:10; John 10:36), and glorified (John 17:5; Heb. 5:9). By the working of the Holy Spirit, through faith, these blessings become ours "exclusively, immediately, simultaneously, and eschatologically in Christ."[50] Through union with Christ, the *ordo salutis*, which belongs in him because of the dignity of his person and work, becomes ours. For these reasons, one should be careful not to equate the gospel (even taken strictly) with justification alone. Justification, like the other blessings we receive, is an applied benefit. Goodwin makes use of a scholastic distinction to clarify this point: "Now the immediate direct end of Christ's intercession is the actual salvation of believers elect, and persons whom he died for. The end of his death is *adoptio juris*, purchasing a right unto salvation; but of intercession, *procuratio ipsius salutis*, the very saving us actually, and putting us in possession of heaven."[51] In another place, Goodwin speaks of salvation by ransom (i.e., his death), power and rescue (i.e., resurrection and ascension), and intercession.[52] So

---

50. Sinclair B. Ferguson, *The Holy Spirit* (Downers Grove, IL: InterVarsity Press, 1996), 102.
51. Goodwin, *Works*, 4:68.
52. Ibid., 4:63.

in relating Christ's death to his intercession, Reformed divines typically distinguish between the means of procurement (*medium impetrationis*) and the means of applying his death to the elect (*medium applicationis*). Thus, for example, the application of justification, properly speaking, is not Christ's death or resurrection, but his intercession.[53] Christ's words "It is finished" (John 19:30) should always be understood relative to his continuing work as the exalted High Priest in heaven. If Goodwin is correct, "It is finished" likely refers to Christ's work of humiliation.

These points only serve to show that the gospel, strictly considered, has in view Christ's mediatorial work from birth (the beginning of his active obedience) to heaven (the continuation of his exalted priestly work). This necessarily means that salvation accomplished and salvation applied are organically related to one another, so that, in the final analysis, the gospel is all that Christ, in his threefold office, savingly accomplishes for his people. Justification, adoption, and sanctification are applied benefits of Christ's work. Once we speak of the gospel in terms of God justifying sinners, we are no less correct to say that the gospel also involves God sanctifying sinners.

But justification, as an applied benefit, does not cause sanctification.[54] As Stephen Charnock argues, union with Christ is the ground of both justification and sanctification, but Christ is the meritorious cause of both.[55] We cannot be justified or sanctified unless we are united to Christ. But it is his person that is the meritorious cause of those two blessings. In other words, one applied benefit cannot be the cause of another applied benefit. Only Christ can cause an applied benefit, whether it be justification or sanctification. The gospel strictly considered has in view Christ's death, resurrection, ascension, and intercession. The gospel largely considered also has in view the application of Christ's redemption, which includes all of our saving benefits. Because of this, both Owen and Goodwin, for example, can speak of the prescriptive part of the gospel since sanctification is the work of God and the work of man (Phil. 2:12–13). It also explains why Goodwin can argue: "If I act anything, it is not I, but the grace of Jesus

---

53. Ibid.

54. This topic has received a good deal of attention in recent years. See Richard A. Muller, *Calvin and the Reformed Tradition: On the Work of Christ and the Order of Salvation* (Grand Rapids: Baker Academic, 2012), chaps. 6–7.

55. Stephen Charnock, *The Works of Stephen Charnock* (Edinburgh: James Nichol, 1865), 3:43.

Christ in me. . . . If I be sanctified it is not grace, so much as Christ, is made sanctification. The truth is, that as a man still grows up more and more gospelised in his spirit, so Jesus Christ is in him, and works out all things else, till there be nothing but Christ in him."[56] With these points in mind, it needs to be said that the gospel, taken largely, in the sense that the Scriptures often talk about, does the most justice to Christ's threefold office as prophet, priest, and king.

CONCLUSION

It may be argued whether this debate is merely about semantics or if there are real differences of opinion on the relationship between the law and the gospel. As noted above, the terms must be explained. Sometimes there is a redemptive-historical contrast between the time of the law and the time of the gospel (WCF 7.5). At other times, those familiar with covenant theology may speak of the law-gospel distinction in terms of the covenant of works versus the covenant of grace. At other times, the distinction between the law and the gospel is understood in terms of whether works are required for justification or not. In this sense, there is an absolute contrast, which was maintained (almost always) by Reformed, antinomian, and Lutheran theologians. But this chapter has raised a further question, specific to the concerns of this book, namely, whether the gospel threatens and commands obedience from believers. Our best obedience may be corrupted, but it is nevertheless acceptable to God because of the mediatorial work of his Son. Even though the gospel commands with the same strength as the law—in fact, some have argued that it commands with a greater intensity because of the indicatives—God is pleased to accept our sincere works of obedience, which, in the context of sanctification, are jewels in his sight. Spirit-wrought obedience includes those good works that God prepared in eternity for us to do as we are conformed to the image of his Son (Eph. 2:10; Rom. 8:29). God justifies the wicked. That is good news. But so, too, is the idea that the wicked are "being transformed into the same image from one degree of glory to another. For this comes from the Lord who is the Spirit" (2 Cor. 3:18).

56. Goodwin, *Works*, 4:339.

At stake is not whether certain theologians and preachers affirm the third use of the law, but what use is made of the law in preaching and teaching, and whether it is presented in all of its aspects: not only as terrible to sinners, but also as graciously guiding the converted—and not only irritating the unregenerate, but also encouraging the regenerate. Especially in preaching, where God's people are gathered to worship, the law should be principally used as a gracious guide to the converted, as Calvin argued. But antinomian theology inverts this order and gives a preference to the terrifying aspect of the law in contrast to the sweet promises of the gospel. In short, the proof is in the pudding. One might theoretically affirm the third use of the moral law and yet preach only the second use.

There have been many controversies on the topic of antinomianism simply because of what people have failed or refused to say, rather than because of what they have affirmed. Our sins of omission are typically harder to identify than our sins of commission, and this is unquestionably the case when it comes to the subject of antinomianism. Thus, as this book has argued, and will continue to maintain, the problem of antinomianism is an acute one. This chapter has aimed to show that the moral law is friendly to the Christian and decidedly unfriendly to the non-Christian. The law is friendly to the Christian only because of Christ's mediation, which makes us friends of God. And the law is friendly to the Christian because it is accompanied by the Spirit, so that our obedience may truly be said to be gospel obedience.

5

GOOD WORKS AND REWARDS

"THESE GOOD WORKS ARE PERFORMED
BY THE FAITHFUL, AND ALTHOUGH THEY
ARE NOT PERFECT, YET THEY MAY TRULY
BE CALLED GOOD, BECAUSE THEY ARE
WROUGHT BY THE SPECIAL MOTION OF
THE HOLY SPIRIT LIVING IN THEIR HEARTS,
AND BY THE ASSISTANCE OF GOD'S GRACE
FROM WHICH THEY PLEASE GOD AND [FROM
WHICH] GOD PROMISES TO THEM THEM-
SELVES A REWARD." —BENEDICT PICTET[1]

REFORMED THEOLOGIANS gave copious attention to the role
of good works in the life of the Christian as they disputed with theologians from other traditions.[2] Wishing to avoid the mistakes of the papists
on the one side, as well as the errors of the antinomians on the other side,
Reformed theologians employed multiple distinctions in order to arrive

1. Benedict Pictet, *Theologia Christiana Benedicti Picteti* (Londini: R. Baynes, 1820), 318–19:
"Hæc bona opera præstantur à fidelibus, et quamvis non sint perfecta, verè tamen dici possunt bona,
quia fiunt speciali motione Spiritus Sancti in eorum cordibus habitantis, et gratiae Dei auxilio, unde
Deo placent, et ipsis Deus mercedem promittit."
2. In the Lutheran tradition, this debate erupted in what is commonly called the Majoristic
Controversy. On this intra-Lutheran debate there is a great deal of literature, but for a good, concise
look at the controversy, see Irene Dingel, "The Culture of Conflict in the Controversies Leading
to the Formula of Concord (1548–1580)," in *Lutheran Ecclesiastical Culture, 1550–1675*, ed. Robert
Kolb (Leiden: Brill, 2008), 39–43.

at a biblically satisfying account of the role of good works for believers. Inevitably connected to this topic is the promise of rewards for Christians who perform good works. The various questions asked in this chapter will focus on the precise issues at stake between antinomian theologians and Reformed theologians.

The issue here is whether good works are "the way of life" or also "the way to life." That is, are good works simply our gracious response to all that Christ has done for us, or are they also a necessary obligation for Christians? In other words, are good works a necessary part of our perseverance in the faith in order to receive eternal life (i.e., glorification)? This brings up the matter of conditions for salvation. Are good works in any way a condition for salvation? In addition, Christians are promised a reward for their good works, but what precisely is the relationship between works and rewards? Importantly, in keeping with one of the major emphases in this book, good works and rewards must find their basis not simply in Christ's power to enable us and reward us, but also in Christ's own life of faith, as he performed good works and received his promised rewards for his faithfulness.

IMPETRATION AND APPLICATION

The distinction between impetration (i.e., Christ's mediatorial work) and application (i.e., the Spirit's application of Christ's work) proved to be hugely useful for Reformed theologians, beginning with Calvin and finding perhaps its most erudite expression in John Owen. This distinction has been mentioned already in previous chapters, but a fuller discussion is required in order to be as precise as possible. Incidentally, not all theologians used these exact terms, but the meaning attached to them can be found as early as Calvin. These two aspects of salvation are organically related to each other, so that what is impetrated by Christ will certainly be applied by the Holy Spirit. In the Arminian schema of salvation, there is a discord between Christ's impetration and the Spirit's application. As already noted in chapter 2, the antinomians essentially blurred the distinction between impetration and application. They were so concerned to maintain the graciousness of salvation that they not only denied that there are conditions for salvation, which was another matter that caused Reformed theologians a great deal of consternation, but also suggested that even in the application of salvation man does not "act" (i.e., he is passive).[3] The Reformed held firmly to the view that the elect have no role in impetrating their salvation. That honor belongs exclusively to Christ. But in the application of salvation, man plays a role. Thus, the application of justification depends on faith. Faith is an antecedent condition to receiving the blessings of justification, adoption, and sanctification.[4]

The nature of Christ's death was differently understood among Reformed, Arminian (i.e., Remonstrant), and antinomian theologians. Christ's death was a work of impetration that could be understood either as a physical cause or a moral cause. In his dispute with Richard Baxter, Owen discusses the differences between physical and moral causes. In his view, "physical causes produce their effects immediately," and the subject must exist in order to be acted upon.[5] Conversely, moral causes "never immediately actuate their own effects."[6] Christ's death was a moral cause, not a physical cause. Thus, those for whom he died do not need to be alive at the time of his death in order to receive the benefits of his vicarious sacrifice. Physical causes do not require human acts, but moral causes do. Moreover, a covenant is required for the effects of Christ's death to take place for the elect. That is to say, Christ's death would be meaningless apart from a covenantal agreement between the Father and the Son in eternity, commonly known as the covenant of redemption (*pactum salutis*). Here we note how important the covenant concept is for Christ's works of impetration.

The temporal covenant of grace is the context in which God savingly relates to individuals. The covenant of grace may be unconditional in its origin, but ultimately it requires that conditions be met on man's part because Christ's death was a moral cause.[7] The covenant is therefore the context in which man exercises faith in order to receive the saving benefits of Christ's works of impetration. The antinomians, wishing to rule out human activity

---

3. On the denial of conditions for salvation, see Tobias Crisp, *Christ alone exalted, being the compleat works of Tobias Crisp, D.D., containing XLII sermons* (London, 1690), 84–85.

4. On conditions for and in salvation, see my chapter in Joel R. Beeke and Mark Jones, *A Puritan Theology: Doctrine for Life* (Grand Rapids: Reformation Heritage Books, 2012), 305–18.

5. John Owen, *The Works of John Owen, D.D.*, ed. William H. Goold (Edinburgh: Johnstone & Hunter, 1850–55), 10:459.

6. Ibid.

7. Reformed theologians have typically distinguished between the covenant as *foedus monopleuron* (one-sided) and as *foedus dipleuron* (two-sided). The covenant of grace, for example, is monopleuric in its origin, but ultimately dipleuric in its execution.

GOOD WORKS AND REWARDS

in salvation, had much in common (ironically) with Baxter and the later hyper-Calvinists by holding to a view that understands Christ's death as a physical cause.

At bottom, Christ's death has to be a moral cause because it is valid for those who did not exist at the time his death occurred. As a moral cause, it works mediately, and that explains why there are covenant conditions. The conditions (e.g., faith) are the instruments by which the moral cause operates.

NECESSARY OR MERELY EVIDENTIAL?

If faith is an antecedent condition required of sinners in order to receive pardon of sins—that is, justification and faith are not synonymous—then, as Reformed theologians insisted, good works, prepared in advance by God (Eph. 2:10) and done in the power of the Spirit (Rom. 8:9–14), are consequent conditions for salvation. In other words, to insist that believers perform good works only as their thankful response to the triune God for all that he has done for them may give the impression that they are not actually necessary for salvation. But as a consequent condition, following from receiving Christ, believers are required to do good works (Rom. 8:13). Again, the error of the neonomians in Scotland was to sneak a good work in (i.e., contrition/repentance) before receiving Christ. But good works are impossible, apart from being in Christ (John 15:5).

Did Rome—particularly their famous apologist, Robert Bellarmine (1542–1621)—correctly understand the Protestant position that good works are merely evidence of sanctity? As far as the Reformed theological tradition goes, the answer is an emphatic no. Rome seriously misunderstood the Reformed, Protestant position. The real point of contention concerns whether, as noted above, good works are the way of life or also the way to life. Adding the latter phrase, "way to life," refers to their necessity. Tobias Crisp, who has been defended by some as generally orthodox and castigated by others for his antinomianism, holds to a view that was rejected by Reformed theologians of his era: "They [i.e., good works] are not the *Way* to Heaven."[8] He refers to the Reformed view as a "received conceit among many persons," namely, "that our obedience is the way to heaven."[9] His rejection of this view may be contrasted with the language of WCL 32:

8. Crisp, *Christ alone exalted*, 46.
9. Ibid., 45–46.

Question 32: How is the grace of God manifested in the second covenant?

Answer: The grace of God is manifested in the second covenant, in that he freely provideth and offereth to sinners a Mediator, and life and salvation by him; and requiring faith as the condition to interest them in him, promiseth and giveth his Holy Spirit to all his elect, to work in them that faith, with all other saving graces; and to enable them unto all holy obedience, as the evidence of the truth of their faith and thankfulness to God, *and as the way which he hath appointed them to salvation.* (emphasis added)

This answer mentions the grace of God in salvation ("freely provideth"), as well as the condition of faith ("requiring faith") in order to receive the blessings, but also asserts that holy obedience is "the way which [God] hath appointed them to salvation." In this schema, good works are consequent conditions of having been saved, whereas in the garden of Eden good works were antecedent conditions to the promise of life.

There is a penetrating discussion of this in a relatively unknown work on justification by John Davenant (bap. 1572, d. 1641). In his disputation with Bellarmine, Davenant addresses the question whether good works are necessary or not. Davenant acknowledges that some "rigid Lutherans" made infelicitous comments on good works, but they were refuted by "our party in this controversy [at Altenburg]."[10] The debate is not whether good works are necessary for believers, but whether they are necessary for salvation (i.e., *vitae aeternae*). Davenant recognizes that the words "for salvation" may pose problems and that they ought to be judiciously used in debates, particularly against Romanists. Nonetheless, after mentioning several ways in which good works are either necessary or not in connection with justification and salvation, Davenant affirms the following proposition: "Good works are necessary to the salvation of the justified by a necessity of order, not of causality; or more plainly, as the way appointed to eternal life, not as the meritorious cause of eternal life."[11] His explanation of this proposition is exceedingly helpful, for he is not speaking about perfectly good works, but about "works of incho-

10. John Davenant, *A Treatise on Justification*, trans. Josiah Allport (London: Hamilton, Adams, 1844–46), 1:293.
11. Ibid., 1:302.

ate holiness, which through the efficacy of grace are wrought by the regenerate."[12] Davenant, while not a Puritan, agrees that, because of the gospel, God accepts imperfect, but sincere obedience (cf. WCF 16.6). At the same time, he rejects the Catholic slander that, in the Protestant view, good works only attest the truth of faith.[13] In short, good works are not only the believer's way of giving thanks to God, but also his duty on the way to salvation.

Peter van Mastricht (1630–1706) also speaks about the relation of good works to justification, which is quite important for the current question. He argues:

> From this come three periods of justification that should be diligently observed here, namely 1: The period of establishment, by which man is first justified: in this occasion not only is efficacy of works excluded for acquiring justification, but so is the very presence of these works, in so far as God justifies the sinner (Rom. 3:23) and the wicked (Rom. 5:5). 2: The period of continuation: in this occasion, although no efficacy of good works is granted for justification, the presence of these same works, nevertheless, is required (Gal. 5:6). And it is probably in this sense that James denies that we are justified by faith alone, but he requires works in addition (James 2:14–26). And lastly, 3: The period of consummation in which the right unto eternal life, granted under the first period and continued under the second, is advanced even to the possession of eternal life: in this occasion not only is the presence of good works required, but also, in a certain sense, their efficacy, in so far as God, whose law we attain just now through the merit alone of Christ, does not want to grant possession of eternal life, unless [it is] beyond faith with good works previously performed. We received once before the right unto eternal life through the merit of Christ alone. But God does not want to grant the possession of eternal life, unless there are, next to faith, also good works which precede this possession, Heb. 12:14; Matt. 7:21; 25:34–36; Rom. 2:7, 10.[14]

12. Ibid.

13. Ibid., 1:304.

14. "Proinde tres justificationis periodi hic diligenter veniunt observandi: nim[irum] Constitutionis, quá primùm homo justificatur: hîc operum, non tantum efficacia ad procurandam justificationem; sed ipsa etiam eorum praesentia excluditur, quatenus Deus peccatorem justificat Rom. iii.23. & impium Rom. iv. 5. 2. Continuationis, hîc bonorum operum, licet nulla admittatur efficacia ad justificationem; requiritur tamen eorundem praesentia Gal. v.6. Et hoc forte sensu, Jacobus nos

This view was not uncommon among Reformed theologians, and Van Mastricht's position establishes both the aloneness of faith as the instrument of justification and the necessity of good works for final salvation. But it is a sign of the times that not a few in the broadly Reformed church today—indeed, even professors of theology—would have a real problem with Van Mastricht's conclusion that eternal life is not granted unless good works are performed by the godly.

Reformed theologians during the post-Reformation era were clear that good works (i.e., evangelical obedience) were not only the way of life, but also the way to life. Witsius comments that the "practice of Christian piety is the way to life, because thereby we go to the possession of the right obtained by Christ."[15] He affirms this point on the basis of the distinction between a right to life and the possession of life. The former (i.e., a right to life) is "assigned to the obedience of Christ, that all the value of our holiness may be entirely excluded."[16] However, regarding the latter (i.e., a possession of life), "our works . . . which the Spirit of Christ works in us, and by us, contribute something to the latter."[17] So much, then, for good works merely evidencing faith.

REASONS FOR THEIR NECESSITY

Like Davenant and Van Mastricht, Anthony Burgess distinguishes between good works as a way or means of salvation and good works as causative or meritorious of salvation. He candidly admits, however, that the human heart does not always understand this subtlety. But he nevertheless also declares that justification apart from the law and good works as necessary

---

justificari negat sola fide; sed opera insuper requirit Jac. ii.14–26. Tandem 3. Consummationis, in quâ vitæ æternæ jus, sub prima periodo collatum, & sub secundà continuatum, ad possessionem etiam promovetur: hîc bonorum operum non tantum prasentia requiritur; sed etiam qualiscunque efficacia, quatenus saltem Deus possessionem vitae aeternae, cujus jus solo dudum obtinemus Christi merito, non vult conferre, nisi, praeter fidem, praeviis bonis operibus Heb. xii. 14. Matth. vii. 21. & xxv. 34–36. Rom. ii. 7, 10." Peter van Mastricht, *Theoretico-practica theologia, qua, per singula capita Theologica, pars exegetica, dogmatica, elenchtica & practica, perpetua successione conjugantur*, new ed. (Amsterdam, 1724), 704–5.

15. Herman Witsius, *Conciliatory, or Irenical Animadversions, on the Controversies Agitated in Britain, under the unhappy names of Antinomians and Neonomians*, trans. Thomas Bell (Glasgow: W. Lang, 1807), 162. Samuel Rutherford likewise says that "holy walking is a way to heaven." *A survey of the spirituall antichrist* (London, 1647), 2:37–38.

16. Witsius, *Conciliatory, or Irenical Animadversions*, 161–62.

17. Ibid., 162. See also Anthony Burgess's excellent discussion of the necessity of repentance in *The True Doctrine of Justification Asserted and Vindicated, from the Errours of Papists, Arminians, Socinians, and more especially Antinomians*, 2nd ed. (London, 1651), 146–54.

for salvation can stand together.[18] Burgess provides thirteen reasons why good works are necessary:

1. "They are the fruit and end of Christ's death" (Titus 2:14).
2. "There is an analogical relation between good works and heaven insofar as God has appointed the way (good works) to the end (heaven)."
3. "There is a promise made to them" (1 Tim. 4:7–8).
4. "They are testimonies whereby our election is made sure" (2 Peter 1:10).
5. "They are a condition, without which a man cannot be saved. So that although a man cannot by the presence of them gather a cause of his salvation; yet by the absence of them he may conclude his damnation: so that is an inexcusable speech of the Antinomian, Good works do not profit us, nor bad hinder us."
6. "They are in their own nature a defence against sin and corruption" (Eph. 6:14–16).
7. "They are necessary by a natural connexion with faith, and the Spirit of God."
8. "They are necessary by debt and obligation. . . . We cannot merit at God's hand, because the more good we are enabled to do, we are the more beholding to God. Hence it is, that we are his servants."
9. "By the command of God" (1 Thess. 4:3).
10. "They are necessary by way of comfort to ourselves. And this opposes many Antinomian passages, who forbid us to take any peace by our holiness."
11. "They are necessary in respect of God, both in that he is hereby pleased, and also glorified."[19]
12. "They are necessary in regard of others" (Matt. 5:16).
13. "Holiness and godliness inherent is the end of our faith and justification."[20]

---

18. Anthony Burgess, *Vindiciae legis: or, A vindication of the morall law and the covenants, from the Errours of Papists, Arminians, Socinians, and more especially Antinomians* (London: T. Underhill, 1646), 37.

19. On God being "pleased" by our good works, see chapter 6 ("Amor, Amor").

20. Burgess, *Vindiciae legis*, 37–46.

Ursinus's commentary on the Heidelberg Catechism presents almost the exact same points as Burgess's work, written decades later in England.[21] Actually, this discussion goes back into the Middle Ages with Bernard of Clairvaux (1090–1153). As Van den Brink notes in analyzing Herman Witsius, "We eat because we live and in order to live."[22] William Ames similarly argues that good works are necessary for Christians because God commands them. More than that, good works are necessary, not only for the good of those inside and those outside of the church, but also as means of glorifying God, "because God is glorified through good works."[23] They are also necessary means of our salvation, "not as a meritorious efficiency, but as a certain disposing presence, in the sense that our election, calling, and salvation appear more certain to us through these good works."[24] In the end, there can be little doubt about the Reformed consensus on this matter. Good works are necessary for salvation. As Owen memorably comments, "It is true, our interest in God is not built upon our holiness; but it is as true that we have none without it."[25]

GOOD OR FILTHY?

Certain verses in Scripture can take on a life of their own, quite divorced from their historical context, and made into the worst possible type of proof texting. Perhaps the most egregious example of this comes from Isaiah 64:6, "We have all become like one who is unclean, and all our righteous deeds are like a polluted garment." Are works always a "polluted garment," "menstrual cloth," or "filthy rags"? This verse is not speaking about good works, but about outward displays of religiosity, as evidenced in chapter 58. To make this verse determinative for how we understand all of

---

21. Zacharias Ursinus, *The Commentary of Dr. Zacharias Ursinus on the Heidelberg Catechism*, trans. G. W. Williard (Cincinnati: Elm Street Printing Company, 1888), 483–88. In the seventeenth century, Francis Turretin also addressed this issue by affirming that good works are necessary for salvation. See *Institutes of Elenctic Theology*, ed. James T. Dennison Jr., trans. George Musgrave Giger (Phillipsburg, NJ: P&R Publishing, 1992), 17.3–5.

22. G. A. van den Brink, *Herman Witsius en het Antinomiainisme: Met tekst en vertaling van de Animadversiones Irenicae* (Apledoorn: Instituut voor Reformatieonderzoek, 2008), 413 (see also 395n2 for Bernard of Clairvaux).

23. William Ames, *A Sketch of the Christian's Catechism*, trans. Todd M. Rester (Grand Rapids: Reformation Heritage Books, 2008), 123.

24. Ibid.

25. Owen, *Works*, 3:576.

our good works goes well beyond what is warranted by Scripture.[26] To be sure, there is no shortage of selective, manageable obedience in the church today that has very little to do with God's Word (see Col. 2:21–22), but the confession in Isaiah does not refer to heartfelt obedience and genuine love for one's neighbor. As Witsius notes, writing in the midst of the late seventeenth-century antinomian controversy, "I judge that the good works of the saints are not intended, in Isa. lxiv.6."[27] But how is a good work to be differentiated from a work that could be described as a menstrual cloth?

According to Burgess, acceptable works are those done by God's Spirit at work in believers. For a work to be good, it must be commanded by God, done by the Spirit of God, coming from an inward principle of grace in a believer, and ultimately done for God's glory.[28] The similarity between Burgess's account of good works and chapter 16 ("Of Good Works") in the Westminster Confession of Faith is obvious. Just as Burgess was writing against the antinomians on this particular point, so too the Westminster divines were determined to set forth a clear-headed discussion of good works in order to combat the errors of the antinomians who appeared to take pride in Isaiah 64:6. They did not do this merely when contrasting the works of the unregenerate to the imputed righteousness of Christ. No one could fault them for doing that, because on that point the Reformed and the antinomians were agreed. But John Eaton, for example, plainly states "that all our righteousness, even of sanctification, is as foul, stained, filthy rags, Isa. 64:6."[29] Hence, Como notes that Eaton's favorite phrase included the words "menstrous rags."[30]

Turretin addresses the question of what constitutes a good work with his characteristic precision. Like Burgess, Rutherford, and the Westminster divines, Turretin affirms that good works must be done in faith (Rom. 14:23), according to God's law, not just outwardly but inwardly as well, and for God's glory. For these reasons, works done in the "flesh" (i.e., as unconverted) cannot be said to be truly good works. The works of believ-

---

26. Are we really to suppose that Mary's "work" in Mark 14:3–6, where she pours expensive ointment on Jesus—an act that he calls "beautiful"—could be described as a "filthy rag"? Nonsense.

27. Witsius, *Conciliatory, or Irenical Animadversions*, 313.

28. Burgess, *Vindiciae legis*, 38.

29. John Eaton, *The discovery of the most dangerous dead faith* (London, 1642), 81.

30. David Como, *Blown by the Spirit: Puritanism and the Emergence of an Antinomian Underground in Pre-Civil-War England* (Stanford: Stanford University Press, 2004), 367. John Saltmarsh also rather enjoyed using this terminology.

ers are good because they are performed "by a special motion and impulse of the Holy Spirit, who dwells in the hearts of believers and excites them to good works."[31] It is actually an affront to God to suggest that Spirit-wrought works in believers are "filthy rags," for these are works that God has prepared in advance for us to do in order to magnify his grace and glorify the name of Christ (1 Cor. 15:10; John 15:5). The truth is, God is pleased by the works of his people. As Turretin notes, "The first cause of their acceptance is Christ, in whom we are pleasing to God (Eph. 1:6) because the person is rather pleasing to God and is reconciled to him by the Mediator."[32]

The fact that our works are tainted with sin does not invalidate them as good works. As Turretin observes, sin is present only "accidentally with respect to the mode, not of themselves and in their own nature."[33] If all our acts were essentially sinful, no one could be justified by faith, because even the act of believing would be sinful. But though there are blemishes in our believing, they do not make believing itself a sin. "Thus the work of faith is not the instrument of justification with respect to such imperfections, but with respect to the act itself."[34] In the Scriptures, then, to be blameless and righteous (Luke 1:6) is not to be sinless, unless reference is being made to Jesus. It is a vain imagination to suppose that we exalt the grace of God by suggesting that the only righteousness pleasing to God is Christ's righteousness. God manifests his grace in providing, not only a righteousness that can withstand the full demands of the law, but also an inherent righteousness that he declares to be both good and pleasing. Not only so, but the grace of God does not end in the fact that he is pleased with our acts of righteousness. That God also rewards the works of believers also highlights the gracious nature of his covenantal dealings with his people.

REWARDS

There is very little preaching in Reformed churches today on rewards in heaven. Our great reward, of course, will be to behold the risen Savior, face-to-face (2 Cor. 3:18; 4:6; Matt. 5:8; Rev. 22:4; 1 John 3:2). But that is

31. Turretin, *Institutes*, 17.4.10.
32. Ibid., 17.4.11.
33. Ibid., 17.4.13.
34. Ibid., 17.4.14.

not our only reward. God will reward our good works (WCF 16.6). Because the works of believers are properly called "good," they will be rewarded. That said, works are rewarded according to the grace of God, not the merit of man (WCF 16.4–5).[35] As Burgess noted above, "We cannot merit at God's hand, because the more good we are enabled to do, we are the more beholding [*sic*] to God. Hence it is, that we are his servants."[36] Or, as Augustine memorably says in his *Confessions*, "We give abundantly to you so that we may deserve a reward; yet which of us has anything that does not come from you?"[37] If a sinner performs any good work, it is because it has been prepared in advance for him to do, and he is utterly dependent upon the grace of God to do it (Eph. 2:9–10; WCF 16.3). But even this point needs to be nuanced, since both the orthodox and antinomians agree on the principle that our ability comes from God.

In addressing the issue of rewards, Owen responds to the criticism that "to yield holy obedience unto God with respect unto rewards and punishments is servile, and becomes not the free spirit of the children of God."[38] Owen could perhaps have listed several prominent antinomian theologians who never tired of making this point. John Eaton, for example, castigates legal preachers for extorting good works out of saints by "hope of rewards."[39] This objection has again surfaced in our day, with even Michael Horton claiming that fear of punishment and hope of rewards, as "*a* sound motivation for Christian holiness" (emphasis added), is a "disastrous pattern of thinking."[40] If fear of punishment and hope of reward provide the

---

35. As Johannes Maccovius says, "In an improper sense you may say that good works will be rewarded." They are not meritorious. For something to be meritorious, four things are necessary: "1. It must be something that is not owed. 2. It should proceed from the powers of those who deserve it. 3. It must be of use to him of whom someone thinks that he deserves something. 4. The reward must not be greater than the merit." *Scholastic Discourse: Johannes Maccovius (1588–1644) on Theological and Philosophical Distinctions and Rules* (Apeldoorn: Instituut voor Reformatieonderzoek, 2009), 251.

36. Burgess, *Vindiciae legis*, 43.

37. Augustine, *Confessions*, trans. R. S. Pine-Coffin (London: Penguin Books, 1961), 23. Heinrich Bullinger (1504–75) shows his dependence on Augustine in his commentary on Romans, where he makes the same argument that our virtue is from God, not ourselves, and so the reward is given to God's people according to grace. Thus, God rewards his own work. See *In sanctissimam Pauli ad Romanos Epistolam* (Zurich, 1533), 37r. Augustine spoke of God crowning his own gifts in the life of the believer in "Grace and Free Choice," in *Answer to the Pelagians IV: To the Monks of Hadrumetum and Provence*, trans. Roland J. Teske (New York: New City Press, 1999), 84.

38. Owen, *Works*, 3:613–14.

39. Eaton, *Dangerous dead faith*, 27.

40. Michael S. Horton, *Putting Amazing Back into Grace: Embracing the Heart of the Gospel* (Grand Rapids: Baker Books, 2002), 80.

only motivation for holy living, then Horton certainly makes a valid point. However, this is yet another area where the Christian life is both-and, not either-or, on the matter of motivation. The fact is, one will have a difficult time finding many classically Reformed theologians denying that Christians should hope for rewards as a motivation for holiness.[41]

Do fear of punishment and hope of rewards cause servile fear in a Christian? Owen asserts that such a reaction is a "vain" imagination.[42] Only the bondage of our spirits can make what we do servile. "But," says Owen, "a due respect unto God's promises and threatenings is a principal part of our liberty."[43] He argues that in the new covenant the hope of rewards, for example, is actually a liberating motive for holiness. Those who are made partakers of the covenant of grace, and make use of the means of grace that God has appointed for believers, may find comfort in the fact that they will not fail to perform the obedience required by God "merely for want of power and spiritual strength" (2 Peter 1:3; Matt. 11:30; 1 John 5:3).[44]

Following from this, the objection may be raised that since God monergistically places us (i.e., by regeneration) in the covenant of grace, apart from any work of our own, we are likewise completely dependent upon him for all of our obedience in the covenant of grace, and so our good works are God's good works and not really our own. According to Owen, while the former premise is true, namely, that we are passive in regeneration, whereby God puts a principle of spiritual life in us, the latter premise does not hold. In sanctification, the grace of God is a work "*in* us and *by* us."[45] Therefore, the strength we have to perform good works in the new covenant "is as truly our own as Adam's was his which he had in the state of innocency."[46] These arguments made by Owen relate to the previous discussion of the "immediate" (i.e., antinomian) or "mediate" (i.e., orthodox Reformed) work of the Spirit as he produces holiness in the elect.[47] The good works of believers are truly the works of people who are active in making

41. Helpful is Francis Turretin's sermon on Hebrews 11:26 concerning Moses' reward. See *Recueil de sermons sur divers textes de l'Ecriture S. pour l'état présent de l'Eglise* (Genève: Samuel de Tournes, 1686), 72ff.

42. Owen, *Works*, 3:614. Note also Manton's comments in *Works*, 5:352.

43. Owen, *Works*, 3:614.

44. Ibid., 3:617.

45. Ibid., 3:620.

46. Ibid.

47. See ibid., 3:625.

use of the means of grace and "answering to the command for universal holiness."[48] Owen adds—and I would say the following quote reveals the genius of his theological mind—that we must avoid two dangerous errors, antinomianism and popery:

> If any such there are, or ever were, who maintain such an imputation of the righteousness of Christ unto us as should render our own personal obedience unnecessary, they do overthrow the truth and holiness of the gospel. And to say that we have such supplies of internal strength as to render the imputation of the righteousness of Christ unto our justification unnecessary, is to overthrow the grace of the gospel and the new covenant itself. But this alone we say, There is grace administered by the promises of the gospel, enabling us to perform the obedience of it in that way and manner which God will accept.[49]

God requires us to be holy. In our response to that command, which we are able sincerely, though not perfectly, to fulfill, because of the gracious nature of the covenant, "we should consider the promises wherewith it is accompanied (among other things) as an encouragement unto the cheerful performance of that obedience which the command itself makes necessary."[50] Rewards, then, are given by God so that we should be cheerful in our obedience, not slavish (Heb. 11:6). With that in mind, Manton makes the salient point that when Christians look to the reward, they "should not look for it as a salary from a master, but as a gift from a father."[51] He further argues that the formal reason behind our good works is obedience to God, but rewards nonetheless act as encouragements. It is true, of course, that "gratitude, love of God and his honour" are the chief reasons for our obedience, but they are not the only reasons.[52]

In heaven there will be different degrees of glory, because rewards differ from Christian to Christian. In addressing this topic, Turretin makes plain that those in the Reformed tradition who hold to "degrees of glory" differ from Romanists regarding the reason why there are differing degrees among the saints in heaven. The difference in degrees of glory does not

48. Ibid., 3:621.
49. Ibid.
50. Ibid., 3:627.
51. Manton, *Works*, 13:458.
52. Ibid., 13:460.

depend on the "unequal merits of men," but on "the mere liberality and mercy of God."[53] But there is some disagreement among Reformed divines on the precise details. Will differing degrees of holiness and the fact that some perform more good works than others have any relation to the rewards they receive? And if rewards are different, will all saints nevertheless be equally happy in heaven?

Regarding the happiness of the saints in heaven, Turretin argues that all will be equally happy.[54] However, Jonathan Edwards (1703–58) disagrees. In his sermon on "The Portion of the Righteous," he argues not only for different degrees of glory, but also for different degrees of happiness. Moreover, he claims that the degrees of glory will be in "some proportion to [the saints'] eminency in holiness and good works" while on earth.[55] Ontologically, there is no reason why human beings in heaven must possess the same degree of happiness. Christ, in his human nature, will have a happiness that exceeds the happiness of his saints. Moreover, there is no reason why our happiness will not increase while we are in heaven. Regardless of the position that one takes, both Turretin and Edwards believe that there is enough scriptural evidence to prove that glory will differ from saint to saint, just as "star differs from star in glory" (1 Cor. 15:41). As Turretin shows, texts such as 1 Corinthians 3:14–15, 2 Corinthians 9:6, and Luke 19:11–26 (see also Matt. 16:27) prove that there is a relation between good works on earth and rewards in heaven. The alternative way to understand these passages would be to suggest that our works will prove to be the meritorious cause of our justification before God. But that option cannot be entertained by anyone wishing to call himself Protestant.

As noted above, the idea of differing degrees of happiness in heaven, while rejected by Turretin, is affirmed by Edwards. Edwards asserts, "It will be no damp to the happiness of those who have lower degrees of happiness and glory, that there are others advanced in glory above them. For all shall be perfectly happy, every one shall be perfectly satisfied. Every vessel that is cast into this ocean of happiness is full, though there are some vessels far larger than others."[56] Indeed, he goes so far as to suggest that the saints in

---

53. Turretin, *Institutes*, 20.10.5.

54. Ibid.

55. Jonathan Edwards, *The Works of Jonathan Edwards* (Peabody, MA: Hendrickson, 2003), 2:902. Turretin's entire discussion on this topic is worth reading.

56. Edwards, *Works*, 2:902.

heaven will be happy that there are others with greater happiness, because sin will be removed and therefore there will be no envy!

To put the matter rather bluntly, there are some Christians who are godlier than others (1 Cor. 3:15). While all Christians are equally justified, Christians are not all equally sanctified. For this reason, those who do more good works than others will receive greater rewards in heaven. Giving a cup of water to someone (Mark 9:41)—or acting in a self-indulgent manner—does indeed make a difference. Of course, there are certain pastoral dangers with this doctrine.[57] Yet whatever pastoral dangers there may be—and there are dangers involved with all points of theology—we are in no position to reject what God has made clear in his Word. And given the paucity of preaching these days on the topic of rewards in heaven, it may not be overstating the case to say that if we deny heavenly rewards, perhaps we think we are wiser than Christ, who speaks openly on this topic in the gospels.

CHRISTOLOGICAL REASONS

In attempting to better understand God's saving work in his Son, Jesus Christ, Christians should keep uppermost in their minds the Reformed maxim that whatever is true of Christ ultimately becomes true of his people because of our union with him. This applies both to his humiliation (sufferings) and to his glory. The fact that Christ went to the cross does not of course mean that we will likewise die on a cross (though some Christians have died that way for their faith). But the Christian life is one of self-denial, in which we daily take up our cross for him who loved us and gave himself for us (Luke 9:23; Gal. 2:20).

Good works were necessary for Jesus if he was to be justified, and he believed the promises that God made to him. At his resurrection, he was publicly vindicated/justified (1 Tim. 3:16) and sanctified (Rom. 6:10). Good works are likewise necessary for our salvation—though, unlike the case with Jesus, not for our justification. Herein is the crucial difference between us and Christ. Moreover, Christ received rewards for his obedience to the terms of the covenant of redemption. These rewards are numerous, such as the promised Holy Spirit (Acts 2:33), the salvation of the elect

---

57. The pastoral issues related to this point are discussed in chapter 7 on assurance of salvation.

(Isa. 49; Ps. 2:8), which includes their sanctification (Eph. 5; John 17) as they bring him glory, and the glorification of his human nature (1 Cor. 15:35–49). Since Christ was rewarded for his good works, his people can rejoice that they too will be rewarded for their good works. In this way, the role of good works and rewards finds its Christological basis, which is crucial to any discussion of applied soteriology.

Writing against the antinomians, Thomas Bedford (d. 1653) makes this precise point, namely, that because Christ looked forward to his reward, believers may likewise look forward to theirs. Far from being a mercenary way of understanding obedience, as the antinomians suggest, this can encourage Christians, as Bedford writes: "Now then if thus it was with Christ, why may it not be lawful for the Christian to help his weakness, by having an eye to the recompense of reward?"[58] Moreover, the saying repeated in some Reformed circles, "God does not need your good works, but your neighbor does," is true enough in one sense. Because of his aseity, God is in need of nothing outside of himself. But Christian theology is not simply God relating to man. God relates to fallen man, in the context of the covenant, in and through his Son. The incarnation makes theology possible since, because of the covenant, all theology is relational. The ontological chasm between God and man is bridged by Christ and the covenant. In light of the incarnation, while the Son, regarding his divinity, cannot have his glory increased or diminished, as the God-man there is a sense in which Christ's glory may be said to increase the more his church is sanctified. Indeed, the more love Christ shows to the church by showering blessings on her, the more he loves himself (Eph. 5:28). This glory, sometimes known as his "mediatorial glory," is not static. It will increase over the ages, until at the consummation Christ will receive the fullness of his glory, when he will publicly present the church to himself in splendor (Eph. 5:27).[59]

To say that God does not need our good works misses the point of Christian theology. Christ requires our good works, not simply as thanksgiving, but out of a necessity that has principally in view his glory as the Mediator who comes to see the fullness of his work as the church is conformed

---

58. Thomas Bedford, *An Examination of the Chief Points of Antinomianism* (London, 1646), 18–19.

59. For a lengthier discussion of Christ's threefold glory (native/essential, personal, and mediatorial), see my discussion in *Why Heaven Kissed Earth: The Christology of the Puritan Reformed Orthodox Theologian, Thomas Goodwin (1600–1680)* (Göttingen: Vandenhoeck & Ruprecht, 2010), 202–21. See also Goodwin, *Works*, 4:349–569.

to his image. The incarnation allows us to think in this manner. In fact, the incarnation requires that we think in this way, so that we will have a proper perspective on why we do good works. To be clear, God does not need our good works, but Christ does, and so he not only requires them, but also desires them. As the Mediator, he ensures that he will give what he commands, so that Christians may bring to him the glory that is rightly his and certainly will be his—because Christ is more interested in our sanctification than we are.

CONCLUSION

The place of good works in the Christian life must be carefully understood. Reformed theologians have gone to great lengths to make sure that the requisite distinctions are in place, so that the truth is set forth and error is refuted. Johannes Wollebius (1589–1629), who studied under Amandus Polanus (d. 1610), states clearly, "The principal, efficient cause of good works is the Holy Spirit in respect of beginning, continuation, and perfection."[60] Their "instrumental cause" is faith, which is the root of good works.[61] As Owen similarly notes, "Faith is the instrumental cause of our sanctification."[62] Wollebius also affirms that these works must be done by regenerate persons in conformity to the commands of God.[63] Wollebius recognizes that they are necessarily imperfect works while we live in this world, but they will be perfect in heaven. Importantly, he argues that the imperfection of our works on earth is covered with Christ's perfection.[64] These good works are necessary, according to "the necessity of precept and of the means, but not by the necessity of the cause or merit."[65] These comments show that there was basic agreement between Reformed theologians on the Continent and in England in the post-Reformation periods. To deny the necessity of good works for salvation is not to promote the

---

60. "Caussa bonorum operum efficiens princeps, est Spiritus sanctus, quoad inchoationem & perfectionem." Johannes Wollebius, *Compendium Theologiæ Christianæ* (Amsterdam, 1655), 216.

61. "Caussa instrumentalis corum, es fides; bonorum operum radix." Ibid.

62. Owen, *Works*, 3:414.

63. Wollebius, *Compendium Theologiæ Christianæ*, 216–18.

64. "Imperfectio tamen haec Christi perfectione tegitur: unde opera nostra semiplena, imò maximis adhuc cum infirmitatibus conjuncta pro perfectis reputantur. Hac ratione de Ecclesia dicitur, quòd nex rugam, nec maculam habeat." Ibid., 218–19.

65. "Necessaria sunt bona opera, necessitate praecepti & medii, non autem necessitate caussae & meriti." Ibid., 219.

grace of God. In this area of dispute, we must emphasize the grace of God in rewarding even our imperfect works. But the reasons and necessity for good works in this life must have a Christocentric basis. Good works were necessary for Christ. Because of the dignity and worth of his person as he performed those good works, he was rewarded accordingly. The same is true for his people. God loves us, and so he rewards our good works, which he prepared for us to do, in order that we might bring glory to God and Christ in this life and the life to come.

6

AMOR, AMOR

**"DIVINES DISTINGUISH OF A TWOFOLD
LOVE; A LOVE OF BENEVOLENCE AND A LOVE
OF COMPLACENCY. . . . GOD LOVES US BOTH
THESE WAYS." —THOMAS MANTON[1]**

A PARTICULARLY COMPLICATED and emotionally charged
aspect of the seventeenth-century debate over antinomianism concerned
God's love for his people. The issue may be stated rather sharply:
does God love all of his people identically, or with the same intensity?
Reformed and antinomian theologians agree that God does not love
all mankind in the same way, otherwise election, predestination, and
Christ's works of impetration would make little sense. The precise
issue in view is whether the elect are all loved equally. In other words,
does God love us more because of our obedience or less because of our
disobedience? During the antinomian controversy in New England, it
was considered unsafe to say, "If I be holy, I am never the better accepted
by God; if I be unholy, I am never the worse."[2] This statement shows
that the debate over antinomianism was not simply about whether the
moral law should be kept or not. While that particular issue was debated,
various related issues also arose, such as whether the holiness of the

---

1. Thomas Manton, *The Complete Works of Thomas Manton* (London: J. Nisbet, 1870–75), 13:140–41.
2. Joseph B. Felt, *The Ecclesiastical History of New England* (Boston: Congregational Library
Association, 1855–62), 1:318.

saints has any influence on God's love for them.[3] Another related issue was whether God is pleased or displeased with his saints when they obey or disobey his law. How does God's pleasure or displeasure relate, then, to his love for his people?

The answer to these questions depends on a correct understanding of God's attributes and affections, as well as—and this is an area that has not received enough attention among theologians—the fact that our relationship to God is in and through Jesus Christ, who is both fully God and fully man in one person. The antinomian view that God sees no sin in the elect means that God could not possibly love his people more or less based on their obedience or disobedience; nor is he displeased with the elect at any time in their life, even before they become believers! But by and large, from the time of the Reformation, Reformed theologians have resisted this type of thinking, and thus have held to the position that in one sense God and Christ love their people equally, and in another sense differently, and thus can be pleased or displeased with the saints.

GOD SEES NO SIN

The idea that God does not see any sin in the justified was a hallmark of antinomian thinking in England during the seventeenth century, especially in the 1630s and 1640s. According to Como, this assertion "was the central pillar in the doctrinal monolith of imputative antinomianism."[4] The antinomian theologian John Eaton explains this doctrine from his "imputative" perspective by arguing that Christ's righteousness clothes believers in such a way that the weaknesses in their faith and sanctification are "covered and utterly abolished from before God."[5] Eaton adds that Christ's imputed righteousness means that believers stand "perfectly holy and righteous from all spot of sin in the sight of God freely."[6] There was no shortage of responses to this view from orthodox Reformed theologians.

---

3. Of course, in keeping with the idea that our good works are prepared in advance by God, we could also look at the issue in terms of whether those who do more good works than others have been recipients of God's love and grace on a greater level.

4. David Como, *Blown by the Spirit: Puritanism and the Emergence of an Antinomian Underground in Pre-Civil-War England* (Stanford: Stanford University Press, 2004), 394.

5. John Eaton, *The honey-combe of free justification by Christ alone* (London, 1642), 127.

6. Ibid.

Not only the polemical Rutherford, but the irenic Sibbes, wrote against this error.[7] The issue is not whether, in justification, God declares us to be as righteous as his own Son. The imputation of the active and passive obedience of Christ, affirmed by almost all Reformed Puritan divines, and, of course, by antinomian theologians, was not debated between them. Rather, the conclusions drawn from this doctrine by antinomian theologians caused a firestorm of debate. For example, because of his view that God sees no sin in the elect, John Saltmarsh reasoned that no sin "can make God who loves for ever and unchangeably, love us less."[8] Again, the problem was not that this statement was completely untrue. But such comments were unguarded and failed to account for the whole truth, which explains why Reformed theologians took issue with the antinomians. In order to formulate a biblically compelling account of how God's love for his people is both the same and different, the nature of his love must be clarified.

GOD'S LOVE

There are different ways of understanding God's love. In the first place, one must distinguish between the intra-Trinitarian love of God and the love God has for his creatures in relation to the affections of his *ad extra* will. God's intra-Trinitarian (i.e., *ad intra*) love is eternal and therefore natural (*amor naturalis*). For this reason, this love is necessary. However, the love of God in relation to his creatures is not necessary, but rather voluntary (*amor voluntarius*). Among Reformed theologians, the voluntary love of God has received the most attention. According to this outward, voluntary love, there is a threefold distinction: (1) God's universal love for all things, (2) God's love for all human beings, both elect and reprobate, and (3) God's special love for his people.[9] This third aspect of God's love—for the elect—"belongs to the category of affection, arising inwardly and extending outward, and is not to be understood as a passion, arising because of some outward good that it apprehends and desires."[10]

7. Samuel Rutherford, *A survey of the spirituall antichrist* (London, 1647), 2:26–27; Richard Sibbes, *The Returning Backslider* (London, 1639), 170.
8. John Saltmarsh, *Free Grace* (London, 1645), 130.
9. See Benedict Pictet, *Theologia Christiana Benedicti Picteti* (Londini: R. Baynes, 1820), 71. "Tres vulgò gradus amoris Dei solent distingui."
10. Richard A. Muller, *Post-Reformation Reformed Dogmatics* (Grand Rapids, Baker, 2003), 3:567.

God's voluntary love, understood as an affection, has three major components. Reformed divines have not always expressed these distinctions in the same way; but the following three categories relate to God's love for the elect: (1) God's love of benevolence (*amor benevolentiae*), understood in terms of God's election and predestination, (2) God's love of beneficence (*amor beneficentiae*), whereby he wills to redeem his people,[11] and (3) God's love of delight or friendship (*amor complacentiae vel amicitiae*), whereby he rewards his people according to their holiness.[12] Staying consistent with their view that God sees no sin in the elect, the antinomians denied this distinction.[13] Rutherford responded to the antinomian denial of a distinction between God's *amor benevolentiae* and his *amor complacentiae* by arguing that "it has an evident ground in Scripture."[14] The antinomians' denial of God's complacent love is "without ground."[15] After providing a thorough explanation of this twofold love of God, Rutherford says that the idea that when a justified person "whores, swears, kills the innocent, denies the Lord Jesus, as did Peter, and David, God loves us as much as when they believe, pray, . . . and God is not a whit displeased with the Saints, . . . is to us abominable."[16] Incidentally, John Gill (1697–1771) rejected this distinction as fiercely as Rutherford affirmed it,[17] though one may question whether Gill accurately understood how orthodox Reformed theologians used it—which is not entirely uncommon in Gill's interpretation of the Reformed tradition.[18] Gill's hyper-Calvinism and avowal of justification from eternity certainly contributed to his distaste for this doctrine. This also shows how similar antinomian theology is to hyper-Calvinism. In the end, the distinction between God's benevolent love and his complacent love has a rich Reformed pedigree.[19]

11. God's love of beneficence is subsumed under his love of benevolence in many Reformed authors, and that is the pattern followed in this chapter.

12. See ibid.

13. See, for example, Samuel Richardson, *Divine consolations* (London, 1649), 207; Henry Denne, *Grace, mercy, and peace* (London, 1645), 32–35.

14. Rutherford, *Spirituall antichrist*, 2:20.

15. Ibid., 2:21.

16. Ibid., 2:22.

17. "It is high time that these distinctions about the love of God, with that of an antecedent and consequent one, were laid aside, which so greatly obscure the glory of God's unchangeable love and grace." John Gill, *A Collection of Sermons and Tracts* (London: George Keith, 1773–78), 3:210.

18. See Joel R. Beeke and Mark Jones, *A Puritan Theology: Doctrine for Life* (Grand Rapids: Reformation Heritage Books, 2012), 141, 147.

19. This distinction is used in the *Acta* of the Synod of Dort: *Acta Synodi Nationalis: in nomine Domini nostri Jesu Christi* (Dordrechti: Isaaci Joannidis Canini, 1620), 49. Thomas Goodwin refers to

Regarding God's love of delight or friendship, Benedict Pictet (1655–1724) argues that this is the love whereby God rewards us for being holy (John 14:21).[20] Besides Pictet, literally dozens of highly regarded Reformed theologians from the Reformation and post-Reformation period made use of this distinction. For example, Melchior Leydekker (1642–1721), a prominent Reformed theologian and professor of theology at Utrecht from 1678 to 1721, also distinguishes between God's benevolent love and his complacent love:

> God's love is either of benevolence or of complacency. The first is the love by which God shall do well to the elect, before there is anything in them that could give Him complacency, John 3:16, Rom. 5:8. And therefore, it can be regarded either as predetermining in God's decrees, or as actually effecting in time. The second, the love of complacency, is the case where God approves the good which is in the elect, especially as being commanded by him and caused, Heb. 11:5–6; John 14:21; 16:26–27.[21]

God's benevolent love is logically prior to his complacent love. It could hardly be otherwise, because God's love of benevolence is the fountain of election and all blessings the elect receive. The love of complacency delights in the good that is in his elect—but that good is only there because of his benevolent love.

A clear statement of God's complacent love comes from Stephen Charnock. He speaks about the implications of believers being more holy, and argues that the more we are like God, the more love we shall have from him. He writes:

> If God loves holiness in a lower measure, much more will he love it in a higher degree, because then his image is more illustrious and beautiful,

---

it as an "old distinction" (i.e., going back to the Medieval theologians). *The Works of Thomas Goodwin, D.D.* (1861–66; repr., Grand Rapids: Reformation Heritage Books, 2006), 1:109.

20. "Primo amore Deus nos eligit, secundo nos redimit et sanctificat, tertio nos sanctos remuneratur. Deo isto ultimo loquitur Christus Joh. xiv.21." Pictet, *Theologia Christiana*, 71–72.

21. "De liefde Gods is of van gunst en welwillentheid; of van welbehagen en genoegen. De eerste is/ waardoor God de uitverkorene wil wel doen, eer dat in dezelve yts in haar is, dat als een zedelijk goed hem kon welgevallen, Joan. 3:16 . . . Rom. 5:8. En zo kan ze of als voorschikkende in Gods besluiten/ of als dadelijk uitwerkende in der tijd werden aangemerkt. De tweede, van welbehagen, is/ waar door God het goed, dat in de uitverkorenen is, byzonder als van hem geboden en uitgewrogt met welgevallen goed keurt. Heb. 11:5/6 . . . Joa. 14:21; 16:26/27." Melchior Leydekker, *De verborgentheid des geloofs eenmaal den heiligen overgelevert, of het kort begryp der ware godsgeleerdheid beleden in de Gereformeerde Kerk* (Rotterdam, 1700), 74–75.

and comes nearer to the lively lineaments of his own infinite purity . . . (John xiv 21). . . . He loves a holy man for some resemblance to him in his nature; but when there is an abounding in sanctified dispositions suitable to it, there is an increase of favor; the more we resemble the original, the more shall we enjoy the blessedness of that original: as any partake more of the Divine likeness, they partake more of the Divine happiness.[22]

Charnock is not merely arguing that God's "increased love" is subjective from our perspective. Rather, he argues that God in fact loves in "higher degrees." In other words, God cannot help but love us more and more if we become more and more like him. Christians will receive "an increase of favor," the more we become like Christ. This view is by far the majority position among Reformed divines from the time of the Reformation onward, but today it is hardly ever discussed or preached on in Reformed circles.

In discussing the doctrine of justification, Francis Turretin notes the language of John 14:23, where Christ promises the love of the Father to those who love Christ, "not affectively and as to its beginning (as if the love of the Father then begins, since he loved us before, 1 John 4:10), but effectively and as to continuance *and increase* because he will prove his love by distinguished blessings and console them by a new manifestation of himself" (emphasis added).[23] The threefold distinction in God's love for his people means that justice can be done not only to texts that speak of God's election of his people (Eph. 1:4–5) and his justifying acts (Rom. 4:5), but also to texts that speak of love in the context of ongoing communion with God and Christ (John 14:21–23; John 15:10; Jude 21).

God's love of benevolence is the ground for his love of complacency. Furthermore, God's love for us must be in Christ. The twofold love of benevolence and complacency is only possible in Christ and our threefold union with the Mediator.[24] God's unconditional love is called his *amor*

22. Stephen Charnock, *Discourses upon the Existence and Attributes of God* (London: Thomas Tegg, 1840), 206–7. Herman Witsius refers to Charnock in reference to God's complacent love. *Conciliatory, or Irenical Animadversions, on the Controversies Agitated in Britain, under the unhappy names of Antinomians and Neonomians*, trans. Thomas Bell (Glasgow: W. Lang, 1807), 177.

23. Francis Turretin, *Institutes of Elenctic Theology*, ed. James T. Dennison Jr., trans. George Musgrave Giger (Phillipsburg, NJ: P&R Publishing, 1992), 16.8.17.

24. By "threefold union," I mean the (1) eternal/immanent union, (2) redemptive-historical /transient union, and (3) existential/applicatory/mutual union. Various terms have been used for each category over the centuries.

benevolentiae; his conditional love is called his *amor complacentiae*. Samuel Hopkins (1721–1803) addresses this point by noting that God's benevolent love necessarily includes his complacent love. "Therefore," says Hopkins, "a complacency and delight in holiness, or moral excellence, is always implied in holiness. God is therefore represented in the Scriptures as delighting and taking pleasure in the upright, in them that fear him and are truly holy, and delighting in the exercise of loving-kindness, judgment, and righteousness."[25] With this in mind, Hopkins makes plain that *amor complacentiae* is not the chief or primary part of God's love, "for holiness must exist as the object of complacency, in order to the existence of the latter."[26] Christians are surely correct, then, to emphasize and glory in God's unconditional, eternal, infinite love of his people. But we are surely correct also to understand that God's complacent love for us has a direct correlation to our godliness. This principle is nowhere more evident than in the person of Jesus Christ.

FATHER-SON LOVE

The love of God for the elect cannot be properly understood except in relation to Jesus Christ. As noted in the introduction, antinomian theologians do not have a robust Christology. God's people cannot relate to him apart from a Mediator. His love for us and our love for God pass through the Son, so that if we love God, we must necessarily love his Son, and if God loves our Mediator, he must necessarily love us. Axiomatic to any understanding of God's love for his people is the fact that the Son, as the eternally begotten of the Father, is, according to John Owen, the "first, necessary, adequate, complete object of the whole love of the Father."[27] Owen adds that in the Son was the "ineffable, eternal, unchangeable delight and complacency of the Father, as the full object of his love."[28] On this point there can be no dispute. But there is more to say about God's love for his Son.

25. Samuel Hopkins, *The Works of Samuel Hopkins* (Boston: Doctrinal Tract and Book Society, 1854), 1:50.

26. Ibid.

27. John Owen, *The Works of John Owen, D.D.*, ed. William H. Goold (Edinburgh: Johnstone & Hunter, 1850–55), 1:144.

28. Ibid.

As the God-man, seated in glory, Christ is still the "peculiar object of the love of the Father."[29] The person of Christ, in his divine nature, is necessarily loved by the Father (i.e., *ad intra* love). However, the love that the Father has for Christ, "as clothed with human nature, is the first and full object of the love of the Father in those acts of it which are 'ad extra,' or are towards anything without himself" (Isa. 42:1).[30] In relation to the church, God "loves him for us all, and us no otherwise but as in him."[31] But there is something else to be considered that more narrowly focuses the discussion of this chapter, namely, whether God's love for Christ is only eternal (and thus necessary) and unchangeable, or whether there is a sense in which God's love for his Son increases in relation to Christ's obedience. In other words, how does God's love of complacency relate to his Son, the God-man, Jesus Christ?

In John 10:17, Jesus says, "For this reason the Father loves me, because I lay down my life that I may take it up again." As Thomas Goodwin notes, "It is spoken in relation unto his fulfilling this . . . command formerly mentioned, so withal imports, *as if God should love Christ the better* for the love he should show to us" (emphasis added).[32] Then, referencing John 15:10 ("If you keep my commandments, you will abide in my love, just as I have kept my Father's commandments and abide in his love"), Goodwin also shows how Christ was commanded by the Father to lay down his life, among other reasons, in order to remain in his Father's love, and that Christ's sheep are mutual pledges of love between the Father and the Son.[33] Again, this love has to do with the *ad extra* will of God with respect to the God-man in his role as Mediator. God delights in his Son, not only necessarily, because he is his Son, but also voluntarily, because Christ obeys the Father perfectly and this brings delight to the Father. It is little wonder, then, that Luke records how Jesus "increased in wisdom and in stature *and in favor with God* and man" (Luke 2:52, emphasis added).[34] If this was true before his baptism, how much more

29. Ibid., 1:145.
30. Ibid.
31. Ibid., 1:146.
32. Goodwin, *Works*, 4:114.
33. Ibid., 4:115.
34. Note also the language in 1 Samuel 2:26 that describes Samuel growing in "stature and in favor with the LORD and also with man."

true was it afterward, as Christ continued in his Father's love by obeying him, even to the point of death!

Thus, the Father has a twofold love for Christ: (1) a natural, infinite, and eternal love of his person, for he is the divine Son, and (2) the love of the God-man, in his mediatorial role, as he obeyed the Father perfectly and learned obedience as he suffered (Heb. 5:8). The former was not subject to increase, but the latter was. This point, not often emphasized when this subject is discussed, has certain implications for our understanding of God's love for his people, which will be addressed below.

Perhaps the fact that nothing in God can be said to be subject to increase—just as there are no attributes in God, but his simple, undivided essence—because there is nothing accidental in him, explains why pastors and theologians do not often speak of God's love increasing. Yet Scripture calls us to speak of God's good pleasure increasing. God had a greater complacency in the completed creation than in the individual parts (i.e., "very good" versus "good" in Gen. 1). God did not change himself, but in the completion of creation there was perfection and harmony of the whole, which indicates that he was more pleased at the end of his creating activity than in the isolated parts before everything was done. God was always pleased with Christ while he ministered on earth, but there is a completeness to Christ's work on the cross—"it is finished" (John 19:30)—that provided the basis for God's new work of creation, whereby he could say it is "very good."

CHRIST'S LOVE FOR HIS BRIDE

The question whether God loves his people in different ways and degrees should never be considered apart from whether Christ loves his people in different ways and degrees. Christ is not only divine, but also human. In his human nature, Christ's love for other humans is subject to increase. Reformed Christology maintains that the finite cannot comprehend the infinite. Christ's gifts and graces (e.g., knowledge, faith, hope, love) increased from the incarnation to his heavenly enthronement and beyond. Indeed, Christ has gained greater knowledge in his human nature in heaven than he had on earth. Moreover, because he received the Holy Spirit afresh in heaven, to the greatest degree possible for a human being, Christ's love for his people increased and did not lessen in any way.[35]

While on earth, Christ apparently did not love all people equally. His choice of disciples was a matter of election, though obviously not in a soteric way in the case of Judas. There is no doubt that Jesus loved all of his true disciples (John 13:1; 14:21; 15:9; 17:9, 12). But there was one special disciple "whom Jesus loved" (John 13:23; 21:7, 20). This disciple was, I believe, John. As William Hendriksen comments, this name ("the disciple whom Jesus loved") "had been given to this one disciple, to him alone. Is it not possible that the others had bestowed this honorable title upon him when they noticed the intimate character of the fellowship between him and the Master?"[36] In his human nature, Christ desired fellowship with other human beings. Just as we experience different levels of intimacy in our relationships, it should come as no surprise to us that Christ experienced differing degrees of intimacy with his disciples. In the case of John, Christ seems to have had a special relationship. The other examples of Mary, Martha, and Lazarus also confirm this point.

Christ's teaching in John 14:21, 23[37] confirms the point about varying degrees of communion. The distinction between God's love of benevolence and his love of complacency enables us to understand the plain teaching of this text, so that the glorious truth of God's unconditional love is not jettisoned for a love that is only conditional. Arminians and Roman Catholics seize upon texts like these and come to numerous unsound conclusions. But, as Turretin noted above, the love promised by the Father and Christ to those who keep Christ's commandments refers not to God's "affective" love (its beginning), but his "effective" love (its continuance and *increase*). Tullian Tchividjian's book, *Jesus + Nothing = Everything*, lacks the theological framework to deal with Christ's words

35. On Reformed Christology, see Mark Jones, *A Christian's Pocket Guide to Jesus Christ: An Introduction to Christology* (Fearn, UK: Christian Focus Publications, 2012); Beeke and Jones, *A Puritan Theology*, chap. 31.

36. William Hendriksen, *New Testament Commentary: Exposition of the Gospel according to John* (Grand Rapids: Baker Book House, 1979), 245–46.

37. "Whoever has my commandments and keeps them, he it is who loves me. And he who loves me will be loved by my Father, and I will love him and manifest myself to him. . . . If anyone loves me, he will keep my word, and my Father will love him, and we will come to him and make our home with him."

in John 14:21, 23 (and 15:10).[38] Tchividjian repeatedly argues that our obedience, or lack thereof, does not affect our relationship with God. His book fails to distinguish between God's love of benevolence and his love of complacency. Moreover, he often states things as either-or, when, in fact, the doctrine in question is more both-and. This approach goes back to the seventeenth century, when antinomian theologians never quite seemed to balance the both-and concept in their theology. Of course, one hyperbolic statement here or there, to emphasize a point more strongly, should not evoke harsh criticism from readers. But his whole book is one lengthy antinomian diatribe, and it bears a striking resemblance to the content and rhetoric of various seventeenth-century antinomian writings.[39]

GOD'S AND CHRIST'S "PASSIONS"

Christ loves his bride, and because he has a true human nature, he has real passions for his church. But because God is simple and without passions (WCF 2.1), he is, as Edward Leigh (1603–71) correctly notes, "neither pleased nor displeased."[40] The Scriptures do, however, speak plainly of God's pleasure and displeasure. Leigh affirms that "God by an external and constant act of his will approves obedience and the purity of the creature, and witnesses that by some sign of his favour, but abhors the iniquity and sin of the same creature, and shows the same by inflicting a punishment" (Ex. 32:10).[41] According to William Ames (1576–1633), when Scripture attributes affections, such as hatred, to God, this must be understood "either as designate acts of the will" or else they "apply to God only figuratively."[42] Simply put, God's anger is an expression of his *ad extra* will, not his essential being. But Christ's anger may be an expression of his person, because he is a complex person (the God-man, who has two natures). Indeed, even in his exalted human nature, as evidenced by some of his remarks to the churches in Revelation (e.g., chaps. 2–3), Christ

38. Tullian Tchividjian, *Jesus + Nothing = Everything* (Wheaton, IL: Crossway, 2011), e.g., 98, 140, 142–43.
39. Readers may be interested to know that the impetus for writing this book on antinomianism came after I had received a startling number of communications from professors, pastors, and layersons in varied theological traditions who had read my online review of *Jesus + Nothing = Everything*. See http://www.meetthepuritans.com/2011/12/16/jesus-nothing-everything-an-analysis.
40. Edward Leigh, *A Treatise of Divinity* (London: William Lee, 1646), 2:75.
41. Ibid.
42. William Ames, *The Marrow of Theology* (Grand Rapids: Baker Books, 1997), 87.

expresses anger. This constant reminder about the person of Christ cannot be relegated to the background. God reveals himself principally in the person of his Son, who is the God-man.

When discussing whether God is angry or displeased, there must be recourse not only to the attributes of God, particularly his simplicity, but also to the person of Christ. Appropriately, Christians may speak about God's anger toward the sins of the regenerate, as well as his delight in their obedience. But in this discussion there must also be a decided focus on Christ's truly human passions as he relates to his church, both in anger and in delight.

DISPLEASING GOD AND CHRIST

Since God's *ad extra* will includes anger toward his creatures, he can in fact be angry at the sins of the elect. The antinomian idea that God sees no sin in the elect had, as noted above, a number of far-reaching pastoral implications, most of which were not very good. One of those was the idea that God could not be angry with the justified.[43] Hebrews 12:5–6, according to "their principles," has in view not the godly, but ungodly persons that need to be chastised in order to be driven to Christ.[44] But orthodox Reformed theologians, such as Rutherford, insisted that God "is really angry at his own children's sins" because he punishes them for their sins.[45] The Westminster Confession likewise makes clear that the elect can be subject to God's fatherly displeasure. Those who are justified can never lose their justification; "yet they may, by their sins, fall under God's fatherly displeasure, and not have the light of his countenance restored unto them, until they humble themselves, confess their sins, beg pardon, and renew their faith and repentance" (WCF 11.5).[46]

In his response to antinomianism, John Flavel deals with the view that God cannot be angry with the elect. He notes that the antinomians are led into this view in part by their fear of popery, and also by the idea that Christ's satisfaction for our sins is inconsistent with the idea that God

---

43. See Eaton, *Honey-combe of free justification*, 120ff.
44. Ibid., 133.
45. Samuel Rutherford, *The Tryal and Triumph of Faith* (London, 1645), 37.
46. Note also answer 48 in the Westminster Shorter Catechism: "These words [*before me*] in the first commandment teach us, That God, who seeth all things, taketh notice of, and is *much displeased* with, the sin of having any other god" (emphasis added).

chastises and gets angry with his people. In response, Flavel argues that God must necessarily hate sin, even in light of Christ's satisfaction. For the Christian, however, God loves the person. "His hatred to their sins, and love to their persons are not inconsistent."[47] Moreover, the antinomians fail to make a crucial distinction between "vindictive punishments from God," which are the effects of his wrath toward the non-elect, and his "paternal castigations," which are the "pure issues of the care and love of a displeased Father."[48]

The differences between the two types of punishments are far-reaching: one is legal, the other evangelical; one is out of wrath and hatred, the other out of love; one leads to destruction, the other leads to sanctification and salvation. Not content with these qualifications, Flavel makes three important concessions: (1) Christ's satisfaction has entirely erased God's vindictive wrath toward the justified. (2) The sufferings of believers are not always for their sins, but sometimes to prevent sin. Sufferings are sometimes for the trial of our graces, and some sufferings confirm God's truths (Acts 5:41). These types of trials "have much heavenly comfort concomitant with them."[49] (3) God's displeasure toward his people, "evidenced in the sharpest rebukes of the rod," does not mean that God's love has turned to hatred. Rather, God's love is unchangeable.[50] In other words, there can be no change in God's *amor benevolentiae*, but God's pleasure, understood also as his *amor complacentiae*, may change. Thus, after the litany of David's sins against Bathsheba and Uriah, we read: "But the thing that David had done displeased the LORD" (2 Sam. 11:27). For believers today, with the incarnation of the Son of God, promise has become fulfillment. There is a heightened indicative in the new covenant and therefore a heightened obligation to love and obey God.

Because of the heightened new covenant indicatives, believers today, when they consciously sin against God's law, not only displease their heavenly Father, but also displease Christ, who reigns in heaven. Christ's

47. John Flavel, *The Works of the Rev. Mr. John Flavel* (1820; repr., Edinburgh: Banner of Truth, 1997), 3:574. Incidentally, the idea that God hates the sin but loves the sinner, which is mocked by many Christians, has a strong Reformed pedigree. God loves the justified person, but hates the sin remaining in the justified person. However, that distinction cannot be made of the non-elect. God hates evildoers, not just evil deeds (Ps. 5:5).

48. Ibid., 3:575.

49. Ibid.

50. Ibid. See also Rutherford, *The Tryal and Triumph of Faith*, 30–43.

displeasure and frustration with his own disciples during his ministry on earth cannot be denied, even with a cursory glance at the Gospels, but in his exalted state the Lord Jesus shows displeasure with, for example, the church at Laodicea (Rev. 3:15–16). Christians need to be warned that they risk grieving the triune God when they willfully sin against his law. While there were and are theoretical antinomians, who deny that God can be angry with those who are justified, perhaps the more pressing problem is that of practical antinomianism, whereby ministers fail to warn their people that they can displease God and Christ or that God can be angry with his people, as he often has been (Ezra 9; 2 Kings 17:18). Equally, there is the other side, namely, that Christians are also able to please God and Christ by obeying their commands and enjoying communion with the three persons of the Trinity.

PLEASING GOD AND CHRIST

Christians are able to please their Father in heaven only because Christ pleased his Father by perfectly obeying him during his earthly ministry (Mark 1:11; Matt. 17:5). As noted above, God loved Christ not only with a benevolent love, but also with a complacent love, far above all men and angels combined. The Father delighted in Jesus, his servant: "Behold my servant, whom I uphold, my chosen, in whom my soul delights" (Isa. 42:1). Because of our union with the risen Savior, Christians are frequently urged to please God and Christ. Sometimes Paul speaks of pleasing God, as in Philippians 4:18 (see also Heb. 13:21; Rom. 14:18; 1 Thess. 4:1). At other times, Paul speaks of pleasing Christ (2 Cor. 5:9). Our conduct may result in being described as "fully pleasing" to Christ (Col. 1:10).

The language of pleasing the Lord helps us to understand the nature of God's complacent love. Speaking of the necessity of good works, Anthony Burgess notes that just as Leah said, "Now my husband will love me" (Gen. 29:32), "so may Faith say, Now God will love me, when it abounds in the fruits of righteousness; for, our godly actions please God, though imperfect; only the ground is, because our persons were first reconciled with God [according to God's *amor benevolentiae*]."[51]

---

51. Anthony Burgess, *Vindiciae legis: or, A vindication of the morall law and the covenants, from the Errours of Papists, Arminians, Socinians, and more especially Antinomians* (London: T. Underhill, 1646), 44.

The Christian, living by faith, continually asks, How may I please the Lord? We make it our aim to please God and Christ and thus bring glory to Jesus, which is his reward for having cleansed us by his sacrificial death. The more we please Christ, the more he comes to delight in his people and rejoice that his work for us is being realized by his work in us. The sanctification of the church is an important part of Christ's glory. It would be incorrect to affirm that we can add to or diminish God's essential glory. But, again, we may or may not bring glory to the God-man, depending on our obedience or sin. Our desire that in all things Christ should have the preeminence should cause us to seek to please him more and more (Col. 1:18).

CONCLUSION

The glorious truth that God loves us unconditionally is a Reformed commonplace that gives wonderful assurance to the Christian. But if this is all that is ever said about God's love, then there is a significant problem, for, as J. I. Packer once quipped in his remarkable introduction to John Owen's *The Death of Death in the Death of Christ*, "a half-truth masquerading as the whole truth becomes a complete untruth."[52] God's benevolent love, which is the highest love that he expresses toward his elect, has not only a logical priority in his twofold love for his people, but also a causal priority. Yet to speak only of God's benevolent love is dangerous, because it ignores the important truth that God loves and delights in the goodness that is in his people, and also the fact that Christ, according to both natures, communes in love with his people, but to varying degrees. The distinction between God's unconditional love, understood as his *amor benevolentiae*, and his conditional love, understood as his *amor complacentiae*, enables Christians not only to make sense of the passages cited above (e.g., John 14:21, 23), but also to rejoice that God is pleased and delighted in the obedience that we offer to him. More than that, the Christological element that has been highlighted in this chapter serves to ground discussions of God's love, pleasure, and displeasure in the person of Christ. As Mediator, Christ was the object of God's twofold love, as well as his displeasure. God was never happier with his Son than when he was angry with him—at the cross.

52. J. I. Packer, "Introductory Essay," in *The Death of Death in the Death of Christ*, by John Owen (Edinburgh: Banner of Truth, 1999), 2.

From our perspective, we relate to God in and through Jesus Christ, which means that when we discuss the pleasure and displeasure of God, we must never divorce that affection from the person of Christ, who, according to his human nature, is necessarily pleased and displeased with his people because of their obedience and sin. To deny that truth would be to rob Christ of his humanity. But his humanity is, for us, as important as his divinity. According to both natures, in the unity of his person, Christ loves his people with benevolence and complacency.

7

ASSURANCE

"I AM NOT AT ALL SURPRISED AT THIS
STRANGE AND ABSONOUS LANGUAGE; IT IS
A FALSE AND DANGEROUS CONCLUSION, YET
SUCH AS NATURALLY RESULTS FROM, AND,
BY A KIND OF NECESSITY, FOLLOWS OUT
OF THEIR OTHER ERRORS." —JOHN FLAVEL[1]

THE DOCTRINE OF ASSURANCE has received copious attention from Reformed theologians.[2] The debates within the Reformed world on this subject have also been examined.[3] Therefore, this chapter will not simply rehash the basic issues that relate to the assurance of salvation. There is the curious fact that theologians have typically missed an important aspect of this subject, namely, the matter of Jesus' own assurance. The manner in which Christ received assurance of his messianic calling is not unrelated to the manner in which we receive assurance of our salvation. So in assessing the basic points of contention between Reformed and antinomian theologians,

1. John Flavel, *The Works of the Rev. Mr. John Flavel* (1820; repr., Edinburgh: Banner of Truth, 1997), 3:590.

2. See the massive bibliography in Joel R. Beeke, *The Quest for Full Assurance: The Legacy of Calvin and His Successors* (Edinburgh: Banner of Truth, 1999), 311–79.

3. See Michael S. Horton, "Thomas Goodwin and the Puritan Doctrine of Assurance: Continuity and Discontinuity in the Reformed Tradition, 1600–1680" (PhD diss., Wycliffe Hall, Oxford, and Coventry University, 1995); Joel R. Beeke, "The Assurance Debate: Six Key Questions," in *Drawn into Controversie: Reformed Theological Diversity and Debates within Seventeenth-Century British Puritanism*, ed. Michael A. G. Haykin and Mark Jones (Göttingen: Vandenhoeck & Ruprecht, 2011), 263–83.

we will attempt to advance the discussion in a Christological direction. We will see that the objective and subjective aspects of assurance are not only necessary, but also complementary to each other. They were for Christ, and they should be for his people.

ANTINOMIAN ASSURANCE

Scholarly works on seventeenth-century antinomianism all give attention to the problem of assurance.[4] The antinomian reaction to orthodox Reformed views on assurance was not, of course, an isolated topic of disagreement. Antinomianism, considered in its seventeenth-century context, whether in England or New England, showed that disagreement on one vital doctrine inevitably led to disagreements on other doctrines. The nature of systematic and confessional theology made this inevitable. Because their view that God sees no sin in the elect was a core belief, the antinomians had to formulate their doctrine of assurance in accordance with it. Their rejection of the idea that God can be pleased and displeased with his people, based on their obedience or disobedience, also had implications for their doctrine of assurance. And their aversion to the necessity of good works, as well as their rejection of the orthodox view of the moral law, caused them to understand assurance of salvation in a manner that was essentially opposed to the Reformed view. One of the major issues was whether sanctification provides evidence of justification.

By and large, the antinomian theologians rejected the idea that believers may be assured of their justification by the evidence of their sanctification.[5] As noted earlier, the New England elders during the theological controversies in the 1630s rejected as "unsafe" the antinomian view that to find evidence of justification in sanctification savors of Rome. Regarding the situation in England, Stoever notes that John Eaton held to the view that sanctification was in itself repulsive to God, but nevertheless assured men of their salvation. Eaton "denied . . . that sanctification is

4. See Theodore Dwight Bozeman, *The Precisianist Strain: Disciplinary Religion and Antinomian Backlash in Puritanism to 1638* (Chapel Hill: University of North Carolina Press, 2004), passim; David Como, *Blown by the Spirit: Puritanism and the Emergence of an Antinomian Underground in Pre-Civil-War England* (Stanford: Stanford University Press, 2004), passim; William K. Stoever, *"A Faire and Easie Way to Heaven": Covenant Theology and Antinomianism in Early Massachusetts* (Middletown, CT: Wesleyan University Press, 1978), passim.

5. See Flavel, *Works*, 3:557, 589–91.

such an evidence to the justified, who rely for their assurance solely on the persuasion that the 'main proposition of the gospel' is effective for them."[6] Moreover, Stoever claims that for Tobias Crisp, "the only adequate ground of assurance is faith in Christ."[7] At bottom, the solution to the problem of assurance was to believe in our justification more. Those who have the strongest assurance are not necessarily those who are most righteous, but those who most strongly believe they are justified. As Como notes, the criticism that emerged from antinomian pulpits and pens was that mainstream Puritans, "instead of promoting justification by faith, . . . instilled a deep dependence on legal works of sanctification. . . . The result was rampant legalism and formalism."[8]

These claims made by antinomians were not entirely untrue. Sometimes well-known Puritan ministers did in fact preach legalistic sermons. Even Thomas Watson was guilty of this. In *Heaven taken by storm* (London, 1669), he explains how Christians must press into heaven with the utmost vigor, but he fails to mention the person and work of Christ. Nonetheless, the antinomians overreacted, and in so doing they committed their cardinal error of throwing out the baby with the bathwater. As will be shown, the Puritans almost always grounded assurance principally in the promises of God. And they did not see such a discord between the works of believers and God's promises. As Joel Beeke notes, "Scholars who assert that assurance is essential to faith in Christ and that sanctification cannot forward assurance in any way are guilty . . . of separating Christ and His benefits."[9]

So averse were the New England antinomians to the idea that good works are evidence of being justified that the New England elders had to condemn the idea that believers know they belong to Christ, not because they mortify the misdeeds of the flesh, but because they do not mortify them, and instead believe that Christ crucified their lusts for them. Rutherford refers to this precise issue in New England and sums up the various ways of stating that position as "to be rich in works of sanctification is to be poor in grace."[10] John Saltmarsh gives a typically antinomian view of assurance

6. Stoever, *"A Faire and Easie Way,"* 141.
7. Ibid., 146.
8. Como, *Blown by the Spirit*, 136–37.
9. Joel R. Beeke and Mark Jones, *A Puritan Theology: Doctrine for Life* (Grand Rapids: Reformation Heritage Books, 2012), 593.
10. Samuel Rutherford, *A survey of the spirituall antichrist* (London, 1647), 2:91.

in *Free Grace*. He is an example of how the radical substitution of Christ in all areas of the Christian life has deleterious consequences for the doctrine of assurance. Saltmarsh writes: "Christ has believed perfectly, . . . repented perfectly, . . . obeyed perfectly, [and] mortified sin perfectly."[11] Thus, with regard to assurance, we must "believe more truth of our own graces than we can see or feel . . . so we are to believe our repentance true in him, who hath repented for us."[12] When this view is understood in relation to assurance, Saltmarsh affirms that a Christian must "see everything in himself as nothing, and himself everything in Christ. . . . All other assurances are rotten conclusions from the Word; and such things as true legal Teachers have invented."[13] More than that, the Christian who looks to his habitual graces, such as repentance, love, and obedience, and not to the blood of Christ, "must needs believe weakly and uncomfortably."[14] Again, this is a classic example of the either-or fallacy. As far as Reformed theologians were concerned, to look at habitual graces as a ground (not *the* ground) for assurance of salvation was not necessarily anthropocentric, but could in fact be Christocentric (Eph. 3:17–19).

The debate between the antinomians and the orthodox Reformed over whether a man may evidence his justification by his sanctification was complex. The issue, as Samuel Rutherford states, is whether we may evidence to ourselves, in our own conscience, our justification by our sanctification.[15] Formally speaking, faith evidences justification. The debate is not whether sanctification formally evidences justification; that is, "Love and works of sanctification do not so evidence justification; as if justification were the object of good works."[16] Reformed theologians did not make sanctification a cause of justification; rather, sanctification inseparably follows justification.

In relation to this point, as noted in chapter 4, the manner in which we speak of justification as the "cause" of sanctification must be carefully understood, especially given its significance for the doctrine of assurance. The antinomians gave a priority to justification that went far beyond what Scripture teaches. That had a number of consequences, to the point that

11. John Saltmarsh, *Free Grace* (London, 1645), 84.
12. Ibid., 84–85.
13. Ibid., 85.
14. Ibid., 86.
15. Samuel Rutherford, *Christ dying and drawing sinners to himself* (London, 1647), 108.
16. Ibid.

justification essentially swallowed up sanctification. In light of this, we cannot deny that our experience of having been justified will assist our sanctification. The fact that the sentence has been passed provides a great motivation for our sanctification and great assurance of our salvation (Rom. 5:1). The existential experience of the believer does not always match up with the order of salvation. Union with Christ is the ground of both justification and sanctification, and Christ is the meritorious cause of both. Just as sanctification does not cause justification, so justification does not cause sanctification, understood in terms of the order of salvation. Sanctification would be utterly impossible, apart from having been justified. But that does not mean that justification, as an applied benefit, can cause another applied benefit. Rather, the peace that we have with God because of our justification enables us to live out the sanctified life as a child of God.

Furthermore, Anthony Burgess, while vigorously opposing the antinomians, nevertheless suggested that the doctrine of justification, unlike any other, inclines God's people to increased humility and self-emptiness, "for by this we are taught even in the highest degree of our sanctification, to look out of ourselves for a better righteousness."[17] Thus, in the matter of assurance, the truth of Christ's imputed righteousness is essential to Christian living, according to Reformed theologians such as Burgess.

ORTHODOX RESPONSE

A summary of the orthodox view on assurance may be found in chapter 18 of the Westminster Confession of Faith. It is an excellent summary of how British Reformed theologians understood the difficult doctrine of assurance. In the first section of this chapter, the Confession notes that those who "truly believe in the Lord Jesus, and love him in sincerity, endeavouring to walk in all good conscience before him, may in this life be certainly assured that they are in the state of grace." These words require some analysis and unpacking. Following the outline of questions provided by Joel Beeke,[18] there are a number of areas in the doctrine of assurance where the Puritans recognized the need to be specific. The first question

17. Anthony Burgess, *The True Doctrine of Justification Asserted and Vindicated, from the Errours of Papists, Arminians, Socinians, and more especially Antinomians*, 2nd ed. (London: Tho. Underhill, 1651), 149.
18. See Beeke, "The Assurance Debate: Six Key Questions," 265–83.

considers whether the seed of assurance is embedded in faith. Faith and full assurance of faith are not strictly synonymous. Our faith does not save; only Christ saves, who is the object of faith. Of course, there is always some degree of assurance in faith, but the main issue is whether full assurance is of the essence of faith.[19] As Beeke notes, "They differentiate between the faith of adherence to Christ and the faith of assurance (or evidence) in Christ, whereby the believer knows that Christ has died specifically for him."[20] The Westminster divines, by noting that infallible assurance does not belong to the essence of faith (18.3), affirm the distinction between adherence and assurance.

The primary foundation for assurance is provided by the promises of salvation. As WCF 18.2 says, the certainty of assurance is "an infallible assurance of faith founded upon the divine truth of the promises of salvation." The Savoy Declaration of Faith and Order (1658) rewords this sentence by adding "founded on the blood and righteousness of Christ, revealed in the gospel," which is more explicitly Christocentric than the Westminster Confession. If God makes a promise, it is yes and amen in Christ (2 Cor. 1:20). One of the "mainstream Puritans" who opposed antinomianism was Thomas Goodwin. He, perhaps more than any other English Reformed divine, gave copious attention to the doctrine of assurance.[21] He discusses a problem that afflicts so many Christians, namely, that they separate Christ's benefits from his person. Christians are in no position to love Christ's work without first loving his person. There is a priority of Christ's person over his work. Thus, Goodwin argues that "whensoever we would go down into our own hearts, and take a view of our graces, let us be sure first to look wholly out of ourselves unto Christ, as our justification, and close with [him] immediately."[22] Goodwin was not alone. The idea that the Puritans "botched" the doctrine of assurance by giving sanctification a priority over God's promises is untrue, and is a claim typically made by those who have not done the requisite reading to be in a position to make such a claim. Goodwin opposed antinomian theology while

19. The connection between faith and assurance is wonderfully described in the Canons of Dort (V.9): "Believers themselves can and do become assured in accordance with the measure of their faith. By this faith they firmly believe that they are and always will remain true and living members of the church, and that they have the forgiveness of sins and eternal life."
20. Beeke, "The Assurance Debate: Six Key Questions," 266.
21. See Thomas Goodwin, *The Works of Thomas Goodwin, D.D.* (1861–66; repr., Grand Rapids: Reformation Heritage Books, 2006), vols. 4 and 8.
22. Ibid., 4:4.

at the same time giving a priority to the person of Christ as the immediate ground for our assurance. To be sure, the antinomians attempted to do that, but only by excising other means of assurance.

The Westminster Confession's teaching on assurance does not simply end with the promises of God as the only ground for assurance. The both-and principle is affirmed, with the idea that God's promises and inward evidences of grace are not opposed to each other (see WCF 18.2, "the inward evidence of those graces unto which these promises are made"). A practical syllogism establishes this point:

> Major Premise: Those who keep God's commandments love Christ.
> Minor Premise: By the grace of God, I keep God's commandments.
> Conclusion: I love Christ.

Or consider how Theodore Beza puts it:

> Qu. But how does a person know if he has faith, or not?
> By good works.[23]

The practical syllogism, however offensive to some, fits perfectly with the teaching on good works in WCF 16.2, where we read: "These good works, done in obedience to God's commandments, are the fruits and evidences of a true and lively faith: and by them believers manifest their thankfulness, [and] *strengthen their assurance*" (emphasis added).[24] In dealing with this point, Rutherford states that God has promised to cause his people to walk in his commandments. "So all the peace we can collect, for our comfort, from holy walking is resolved on a promise of free-grace, and the duty as performed by the grace of the covenant, may and does lead us to the promise and no wise from Christ but to Christ."[25]

Besides the practical syllogism, the Westminster Confession also affirms what has been called a "mystical syllogism." Beeke sets forth a type of mystical syllogism:

---

23. Cited in Richard A. Muller, *Calvin and the Reformed Tradition: On the Work of Christ and the Order of Salvation* (Grand Rapids: Baker Academic, 2012), 258.

24. See also Heidelberg Catechism, Q & A 86 (Lord's Day 32), "... so that we may be assured of our faith by its fruits."

25. Samuel Rutherford, *The Tryal and Triumph of Faith* (London, 1645), 183.

Major Premise: According to Scripture, only those who possess saving faith will so experience the Spirit's confirmation of inward grace and godliness that self decreases and Christ increases.

Minor Premise: I cannot deny that by the grace of God I experience the Spirit's testimony confirming inward grace and godliness such that self decreases and Christ increases.

Conclusion: I am a partaker of saving faith.[26]

This type of reasoning is also present in the Westminster Confession (18.2), where assurance is grounded in the promises of God and "the inward evidence of those graces unto which these promises are made, the testimony of the Spirit of adoption witnessing with our spirits that we are the children of God." Thus, Beeke is surely correct to argue that the "best resolution of the objective-subjective tension in assurance is that both owe everything to Christ, receive all from Him, and end with all in Him. In Christ, objective promises and subjective experience are complementary."[27] Christ is not only for us (i.e., objective), but also in us, the hope of glory (i.e., subjective). In connection with this, Richard Muller makes a number of important observations regarding Beza's doctrine of assurance. He particularly contends that Beza, like Calvin, "did anchor assurance in Christ and, specifically, in union with Christ. Arguably the basic point made by Calvin and shared by Beza was that the basis for personal assurance is not Christ standing *extra nos* in the sufficiency of his saving work, but rather personal or subjective recognition of the effects of Christ and his work in the believer as the basis for assurance."[28] Thus, a focus on good works as a ground for assurance of faith does not necessarily turn the believer away from Christ. Good works may enable the believer to subjectively focus on the work of Christ in him or her. Subjective assurance necessarily takes place in the life of the believer because Christ's work is not only objective, but also subjective. Indeed, as we are about to see, even Christ's own assurance was both objective and subjective, with both complementing each other in the most perfect way.

26. Beeke, "The Assurance Debate: Six Key Questions," 274.
27. Ibid., 276.
28. Muller, *Calvin and the Reformed Tradition*, 267.

CHRIST'S ASSURANCE

As noted above, the topic of Christ's own personal assurance does not receive much, if any, attention in discussions of assurance. Obviously, Christ's assurance and our assurance are not strictly the same. He is the Savior; we are the saved. But that does not mean that there are not parallels that help us in framing a biblically coherent doctrine of assurance.

Christ trusted in the promises of God (Isa. 49:1–7); he was, as Goodwin claims, "the highest instance of believing that ever was."[29] As the faithful, obedient servant of the Lord, Jesus looked to many promises made to him by the Father. From the gift of the Spirit to the inheritance of the nations to the name that is above every name, Christ received assurance from his Father that the promises made to him would one day (after his resurrection) be his. Not only that, but Christ was obedient, and his obedience would naturally have assured him of his messianic calling as the second Adam. Whether reading as a young man the third servant song in Isaiah (50:4–9) or daily committing himself to the Father (Ps. 31:5), which culminated at his death (Luke 23:46), Christ was assured of his special task because of inward graces. Indeed, as John writes in his gospel, Jesus kept his Father's commandments, and so abode in his love (15:10). In addition, Christ would have had a healthy fear of the Lord, knowing that if he shrank back just once, his Father would not have been pleased with him (Heb. 10:38). Assurance, for Christ, was not simply looking to the promises, but also looking to the inward graces communicated to his human nature by the Holy Spirit.

More than that, returning to the objective side, Christ received assurance at his baptism and at the Transfiguration (Mark 1:9–11; 9:2–8). The Father assured Jesus that he was God's Son, and was well pleasing to him. But Christ would also have received assurance that he was God's Son in the subjective realm as he prayed. Surely what is true of believers, namely, that the Spirit enables us to cry "Abba, Father" (Rom. 8:15–16), is true of the man who was endowed with the Spirit above measure (John 3:34). It was as natural for Jesus to cry "Father" during his times of prayer—indeed, the course of his life, even right before his death, shows this to be true—as

---

29. Goodwin, *Works*, 4:9. Goodwin also comments, "Christ thus trusted God upon his single bond; but we, for our assurance, have both Christ and God bound to us." Ibid.

it was for him to breathe. In addition, there can be little doubt that every time that Christ prayed, he was assured of his special relationship with his Father in heaven. As Sinclair Ferguson notes, the Spirit of sonship and assurance bore witness with Christ's spirit that he was the Messiah: "The Spirit thus seals and confirms the bond of love and trust between the Father and the incarnate Son."[30]

Believers are commanded to look to Christ for their assurance, and rightly so. If the foregoing has any merit, we may be assured of our salvation, not only because of the beauty and excellence of his person and work, but also by looking to his life as a pattern of how we may likewise be assured of our eternal destiny. To the degree that we look to Christ for us and in us, including his example to us in his earthly sojourn, we will find ourselves not only assured that we are the children of God, but also convinced that the objective-subjective approach to assurance is more Christ-centered than perhaps initially thought.

MULTIFACETED, CHRISTOCENTRIC ASSURANCE

Just as Christ's assurance was multifaceted, so the believer will also experience assurance of salvation in many different ways. The promises of God, which are many (literally hundreds), assure Christians that, for example, nothing can separate them from the love of God (Rom. 8:31–39). The promises of God require, moreover, that his people look to the person and work of Christ. Some Christians lack assurance because they have an inadequate understanding of Christology. Not only that, but a failure to understand and love God's attributes, such as his wisdom, immutability, power, and goodness, will also lead to a lack of assurance. These attributes, which are all harmonious with one another, so that, for example, his immutability is his goodness, and vice versa, should provide Christians with the assurance that God's love for them cannot change because God cannot change. On the subjective side, obeying God's commandments (1 John 2:3–6), which necessarily includes loving God and his people (1 John 3:11–24), cannot but aid a believer in the quest for full assurance. To deny this would be to overthrow the Christian religion. Connected with that, Christians who pray receive the Spirit of adoption,

30. Sinclair B. Ferguson, *The Holy Spirit* (Downers Grove, IL: InterVarsity Press, 1996), 47.

which enables them to cry—as Christ cried out on the cross (Matt. 27:50, where the same Greek word, *krazein*, is used)—"Abba! Father!" (Rom. 8:15–16). Christians who struggle with their lack of faith should also be reminded that their struggle with unbelief is a sign of belief (Mark 9:24). It may seem obvious to most, but unbelievers do not struggle with unbelief; Christians do, however, because they are concerned that their faith wavers. Moreover, the point should be made that our worship experience should incorporate all that has been said about how to attain assurance. Specifically, Christians should sing, not only good hymns, but especially the Psalms, for in singing many of the psalms you are left with little doubt whose side you are on!

There is another important aspect of assurance that is rarely touched upon by pastors and theologians. The person of Christ, in his heavenly ministry as our sympathetic high priest (Heb. 4:14–15), has much value to the Christian who seeks assurance of salvation. The incarnation of the Son of God enabled God to be compassionate and merciful in a manner that would have been impossible had the Son not assumed a human nature. As Thomas Goodwin remarks, "His taking our nature at first clothed with frailties, and living in this world as we, this has forever fitted his heart by experience to be in our very hearts and bosoms; and not only or barely to know the distress . . . but experimentally remembering the like in himself once."[31] Because the Son has a true human nature, he had affections and experiences that were proper to that nature in the context in which he lived. He also remembers those experiences, even now in his exalted state in heaven (Heb. 5:7–10). But because Christ is exalted, having received the gift of the Spirit in the greatest measure possible for a human being, the fruit of the Spirit (love, joy, peace, etc.) in his human nature are greater in heaven than they were on earth. These truths about Christ's person in heaven are invaluable for the believer. As Goodwin notes, our sins "move him to pity more than to anger."[32] Goodwin continues:

31. Goodwin, *Works*, 4:141.
32. Ibid., 4:149. James Durham rightly says that many Christians are ignorant of the value of Christ's intercession. Taking a view similar to Goodwin's, he writes: "We will find that this intercession and sympathy is not broken off and made less because of the believer's sin; but is in some respect the more stirred and provoked, because this sympathy flows from the relation that is between Head and members, which sin does not cut off; and it is as with a tender natural parent, who cannot but be affected with the child's straits, even though he has shamefully brought them on himself; yes, his very failings do touch and affect: so our high Priest's sympathy, is not only in crosses, but it is to have pity

107

> The object of pity is one in misery whom we love; and the greater the misery is, the more is the pity when the party is beloved. Now of all miseries, sin is the greatest. . . . And [Christ], loving your persons, and hating only the sin, his hatred shall all fall, and that only upon the sin, to free you of it by its ruin and destruction, but his bowels shall be the more drawn out to you; and this as much when you lie under sin as under any other affliction.[33]

Christians live with the ugly reality of their sin on a daily basis. In fact, in some respects, our sin is worse than the sins of unbelievers, for we have greater knowledge and greater powers to resist.[34] But believers must know, based on Christ's office as priest in his exalted state, that Jesus feels more pity than anger toward us as sinners.

There are a number of "ordinary means" in which believers may gain infallible assurance of faith (WCF 18.3). God's objective promises should always be uppermost in our minds, for without them the subjective elements of assurance would be impossible. But there is the real danger of making these two elements enemies, when in fact they are friends because Christ and his benefits are friends. All of this shows that the Christian life is complex. Calls to trust God, who justifies the wicked, are essential to the pastoral ministry, but if that is all that preachers speak about with regard to assurance, then they are preaching like antinomians. And, I would say, they are pastorally insensitive to the fact that God is gracious and has given his people many means by which they may have the infallible assurance of salvation, which God and Christ desire for all their people. More than that, preachers have a duty to preach the whole Christ. So many stop at his death, and remind their people that Christ uttered the words, "It is finished," but the better way is to preach not only Christ's death and resur-

---

on the ignorant, and compassion on these that are out of the way, Heb. 5. And thus the very sin of a believer affected Him so, that He cannot but sympathize and be provoked to sympathize with him. O what a wonder is this, the more sin, the more sympathy! which ought to make believers humble, and yet exceedingly to comfort them under a sinful condition." *A Commentarie upon the Book of the Revelation* (Amsterdam, 1660), 411.

33. Goodwin, *Works*, 4:149.

34. Johannes Maccovius also points out that unbelievers sin more seriously insofar as they "rush into sin with great desire, [but] believers with a broken will; . . . the faithful feel sadness about their committed sins, unbelievers are pleased by them." *Scholastic Discourse: Johannes Maccovius (1588–1644) on Theological and Philosophical Distinctions and Rules* (Apeldoorn: Instituut voor Reformatieonderzoek, 2009), 193.

rection, but also his intercessory work as our merciful high priest. Again, the antinomian error is one of failing to do justice to the totality of Christ's person and work. It is, above all, a Christological error.

CONCLUSION

Reformed and antinomian theologians have significantly different views regarding assurance. However, the question of assurance spills over into Christology. Christology, including Christ's own experience as God's servant on earth, has much to teach us about the multifaceted nature of assurance. Besides that, Christ's own role as a merciful high priest gives believers abundant reason to believe that Christ is even more merciful to his bride while he is in heaven than when he was on earth. These Christological truths are often completely missed by pastors with antinomian tendencies. In their desire to exalt Christ, they often fail to do just that. Antinomian preaching in the past and today often fails to extol the grace of the gospel extensively enough. They diminish the power of the gospel and vitiate the glory of Christ in large measure.

The debate between the two parties was never, as Rutherford notes, "touching the first assurance of justification"; it was axiomatic to Reformed theology that believers are first assured of their justification by faith, not by good works.[35] However, that does not mean, of course, that good works play no role in assurance. The antinomians could not give a role to good works in assurance, other than to say that they are frequently dangerous signs, because of their denial of conditions in the covenant of grace, their view that Christ repented, believed, etc., for his people, and their view that God sees no sin in his people. In doing this, they went too far. But Reformed theologians were sensitive to the dangers of their own "qualifications." Nonetheless, that did not stop them from affirming that good works are a lawful means for attaining assurance. As Flavel says in his response to this particular antinomian error,

> I will further grant, That the eye of a Christian may be too intently fixed upon his own gracious qualifications; and being wholly taken up in the reflex acts of faith, may too much neglect the direct acts of faith upon Christ, to the great detriment of his soul.

35. Rutherford, *Christ dying and drawing sinners*, 110.

109

But all this notwithstanding, The examination of our justification by our sanctification, is not only a lawful, and possible, but a very excellent and necessary work and duty. It is the course that Christians have taken in all ages, and that which God has abundantly blessed to the joy and encouragement of their souls.[36]

The truth is, to the degree that a person fixes his or her eyes upon Christ, he or she will burst forth with gospel obedience. And obedience, if it is gospel obedience, cannot help but draw us back to Christ in faith, hope, and love. For this reason, the objective and subjective aspects of the Christian life are complementary and necessary. Indeed, by looking inward, Christians may trace the hand of God in their lives and return in thanksgiving and praise. To say "Just look to Christ" does not mean that we should not look inward, for Christ dwells in our hearts by faith (Eph. 3:17).

36. Flavel, *Works*, 3:590. Reformed divines typically speak of a "double act of faith." The direct act of faith refers to the person's act of relying upon the promises of God in Christ. The reflex act of faith enables the person to look at a subjective work (e.g., love for neighbor) and thereby gain assurance. As Flavel notes elsewhere, "The soul has not only power to project, but a power also to reflect upon its own actions; not only to put forth a direct act of faith upon Jesus Christ, but to judge and discern that act also." Ibid., 2:330.

8
RHETORIC

"ANTINOMIANS MAKE ALL DUTIES A MATTER OF COURTESY."—SAMUEL RUTHERFORD[1]

RHETORIC IS A POWERFUL weapon in theological debate. Its effectiveness does not necessarily imply that the rhetoric was accurately or judiciously used. But that rarely matters to the "winner." The rhetoric that flew back and forth between antinomian and Reformed theologians in the seventeenth century may explain why there are not too many books on antinomianism, even today when one might expect some.

Those who defend or are at least sympathetic to the antinomians will typically refer to them as "the so-called antinomians," not wanting to attribute the hostile epithet "antinomian" to them. Sometimes they will say that the antinomians were simply trying to lead their people to Christ. And with such a noble goal, who could fault them for exalting the free grace of Jesus Christ?

What is more, given that most people understand antinomianism etymologically as being simply "against the law," without appreciating its full theological significance in the seventeenth century, they vindicate most antinomians as basically orthodox. For example, Tobias Crisp not only made a number of orthodox statements, but also spoke positively about obedience in the Christian life. That is enough, for some (e.g., John Gill), to dismiss the idea that he was an antinomian or heterodox—though it does make

1. Samuel Rutherford, *A survey of the spirituall antichrist* (London, 1647), 2:29.

111

for painful reading at times when Gill tries to explain and qualify Crisp's thought. Crisp was often guilty of speaking out of both sides of his mouth. He also affirmed a number of unorthodox views, such as justification at birth (i.e., before faith), the rejection of good works as necessary for salvation, and the view that at the cross Christ became the greatest sinner that ever lived. These views alone had other consequences for his theology, and there were a number of gross inconsistencies that emanated from his pen. It was not one idiosyncrasy, but several, that made Crisp suspect to the majority of Reformed divines in the 1640s. But does he deserve the title "antinomian"? That depends, of course, on how the term is defined. Crisp was not as radical as some antinomians in the seventeenth century, but he made a number of careless and provocative statements, besides holding to some rather odd views. That seems to explain why the Westminster divines were, by and large, quite suspicious of his work.

Whatever the assessment, the example of Crisp shows how complex the situation was in England during the 1640s and, indeed, when his sermons were reprinted toward the end of the seventeenth century. Hostile remarks were aimed by Reformed theologians at a number of heterodox groups (e.g., Arminians, Socinians, Quakers, and antinomians), but it was certainly not a one-way street. This chapter will look at some of the rhetoric that was used during the antinomian debates in the 1600s, and also make some application to today's church.

THE NINTH COMMANDMENT

The Westminster Larger Catechism provides an important exposition of the duties that are required by the ninth commandment. Those duties include the "preserving and promoting of truth between man and man, and the good name of our neighbour, as well as our own; appearing and standing for the truth; and from the heart, sincerely, freely, clearly, and fully, speaking the truth, and only the truth, in matters of judgment and justice, and in all other things whatsoever; a charitable esteem of our neighbours; loving, desiring, and rejoicing in their good name; sorrowing for, and covering of their infirmities; freely acknowledging of their gifts and graces, defending their innocency; a ready receiving of a good report, and unwillingness to admit of an evil report, concerning them; discouraging tale-bearers, flatterers, and slanderers; love and care of our own good name, and defending it when need requireth; keeping of lawful promises; studying and practising of whatsoever things are true, honest, lovely, and of good report" (WLC 144). Without doubt, Reformed and antinomian theologians did not always keep the ninth commandment perfectly or even well when it came to their polemical debates. Rutherford's zeal seems to have gotten the better of him at times; he did not always charitably read his opponents, though many of his general concerns appear to be correct. But Isaac Chauncy seems to have provided an unfair and harsh assessment of Daniel Williams in *Neonomianism unmask'd, or, The ancient gospel pleaded against the other, called a new law or gospel in a theological debate, occasioned by a book lately wrote by Mr. Dan. Williams* (London, 1692). Baxter may have been a "neonomian," but Williams was not (contra Chauncy).

The fact remains, however, that not just Rutherford, but literally dozens of well-known Reformed theologians in England, New England, and on the Continent, opposed antinomianism. Were Rutherford, Flavel, Burgess, Owen, Goodwin, Sibbes, and the like all wrong about the errors of antinomianism? Did they all misread the writings of authors such as Eaton, Towne, Crisp, and Traske? Theoretically, that is possible, but it is unlikely. The duties of the ninth commandment, which the divines would have been keenly aware of, both in their minds and in their hearts, bound them in their conduct toward other theologians, but not in a way that would compromise duties required of them by the first and third commandments (see WLC 104–5, 112–13).

DIFFERENT TYPES OF ACCUSATIONS

Different types of accusations emerged during the antinomian crises in the seventeenth century. As noted in chapter 1, the antinomian theologians accused a number of preachers of being legalists because they did not preach enough on the faith of free justification. According to John Eaton, these preachers "are exceeding dangerous, as by a preposterous zeal of works and well-doings, speak little or nothing of faith of free justification. . . . Instead of making them the children of the promise, they make them children that will be under the Law and works, Gal. 4.21. Instead of making them children of faith and of the blessing, they make them the children of works and of the curse, Gal. 3.10. Instead of working peace with God in their consciences, they work unquietness, fears, and troubles of conscience about works."[2] However, the Reformed theologian Thomas Blake (1596/7–1657) writes with equal fury against the antinomians: "But the severing of the promise from the duty, so that Christ is heard only in a promise, not at all in a precept, when they hear that Christ will save; but are never told that they must repent. These are but delusions; Promise-Preachers, and no duty-Preachers; grace-Preachers, and not repentance-Preachers, do but . . . deceive with vain words, Eph. 5:6."[3] Examples such as these from both sides could be multiplied. But there are some comments from Burgess, which he makes in his work against the antinomians, that are worthy of further reflection.

In the first place, he notes quite early on in *Vindiciae legis* that the antinomian "may set up his preaching of grace, as a work more eminent, and so trust to that more than Christ."[4] This comment is actually quite perceptive. There is today a great deal of talk about "grace." It is described as scandalous, liberating, shocking, counterintuitive, unpredictable, dangerous, etc. But when an emphasis on grace eclipses a focus on Christ, as it sometimes does, then grace is not being preached; rather, a sort of cheerleading experience takes place, in which very little is actually said about grace because it is divorced from the richness of Christ's person and work.

Burgess also notes that his acquaintance with the antinomians comes through their books. But the errors in their books are "more warily dressed than in secret. There I find, that sometimes they yield the law to be a rule of life, yea, they judge it a calumny to be called Antinomists; and if so, their adversaries may be better called Antifidians. And it cannot be denied, but that in some parts of their books there are wholesome and good passages . . . yet for all this, in the very places where they deny this assertion as theirs, they must be forced to acknowledge it. The Author of the *Assertion of Free grace*, who does expressly touch upon these things, and disclaims the opinion against the law, page 4 and page 6, yet he affirms there such principles, from whence this conclusion will necessarily follow."[5]

2. John Eaton, *The discovery of the most dangerous dead faith* (London, 1642), 191–94.

3. Thomas Blake, *Vindiciæ Foederis* (London, 1658), 189.

4. Anthony Burgess, *Vindiciae legis: or, A vindication of the morall law and the covenants, from the Errours of Papists, Arminians, Socinians, and more especially Antinomians* (London: T. Underhill, 1646), 16.

5. Ibid., 268–69.

These comments from Burgess show how truly difficult it is to pinpoint an antinomian—difficult, but not impossible.

Robert Towne, who authored the book that Burgess refers to above, claims in his response to Burgess that true believers walk according to the rule of the law, "yet it is not by virtue from the Law regulating him, but from another power within, renewing and disposing the heart thereunto."[6] This is classic antinomian rhetoric. Antinomians wish to avoid the idea that believers can do whatever they please, which would be practical antinomianism, but they try with all their might to avoid speaking positively about the law as a rule or guide for believers. Similarly, John Eaton claims that the law should not be a rule in the conscience of a believer, "especially seeing it cost so great a price to deliver the conscience from the Schoolmaster-like slavery of the Law; let the godly learn therefore, that the Law and Christ are two contrary things, whereof the one cannot abide the other; for when Christ is present, the Law may in no case rule, but must depart out of the conscience."[7] As already noted in this book, the antinomians gave such a hermeneutical and practical priority to the doctrine of justification that they were loath to speak about the moral law in a positive sense. The Upper Room discourse teaches us many things, including the idea that Christ is the new Moses, the new lawgiver. To eradicate the moral law from the conscience of the Christian is to attempt to eradicate Christ himself. Christ was a walking transcript of the law while on earth; therefore, failing to love the law of God is failing to love Christ himself.

This book has argued that what make the antinomians so dangerous are the subtleties of their errors. David Como perceptively remarks that there "were few statements made by the Eatonists that cannot be found duplicated elsewhere, at some point, and under some other circumstances by impeccably respectable English godly sources. It was not the matter of Eatonist thought which made it so controversial; rather, it was the arrangement of the matter, the subtle shifts in meaning, and most of all, the uses to which the Eatonists put their newly constructed system that separated them from their puritan opponents."[8] One has to read carefully to see the

6. Robert Towne, *A Re-assertion of Grace . . . A Vindication of the Gospel-truths, from the unjust censure and undue aspersions of Antinomians* (London, 1654), 139.

7. John Eaton, *The honey-combe of free justification by Christ alone* (London, 1642), 449.

8. David Como, *Blown by the Spirit: Puritanism and the Emergence of an Antinomian Underground in Pre-Civil-War England* (Stanford: Stanford University Press, 2004), 207.

subtle shift that took place from Reformed orthodoxy to antinomianism. Indeed, it is not uncommon to find readers in the past and in the present confess that they see little wrong with the thought of those whom I would describe as antinomian.

Tullian Tchividjian commits the same errors as many seventeenth-century antinomians. He holds that "sanctification is the daily hard work of going back to the reality of our justification."[9] This way of theologizing impacts his exegesis of Philippians 2:12–13. According to Tchividjian, "We've got work to do—but what exactly is it? Get better? Try harder? Pray more? Get more involved in church? Read the Bible longer? What precisely is Paul exhorting us to do?" Tchividjian's answer: "God works his work in you, which is the work already accomplished by Christ. Our hard work, therefore, means coming to a greater understanding of his work."[10] How does this fit with Paul's exhortation to work out our salvation with fear and trembling? Paul surely did not reduce Christian living to contemplating Christ—after all, in 1 Thessalonians 5, toward the end of the chapter, Paul lists over fifteen imperatives. But Tchividjian's type of antinomian-sounding exegesis impacts churches all over North America. Of course, he also uses antinomian-sounding rhetoric himself. In his view, "a lot of preaching these days has been unwittingly, unconsciously seduced by moralism." He adds, "So many contemporary sermons strengthen this slavery to self. 'Do more, try harder' is the constant refrain." In fact, "Many sermons today provide nothing more than a 'to do' list. . . . It's all law (what we must do) and no gospel (what Jesus has done)."[11] This may well be true, though I suspect that the last part is overstated. But Tchividjian's theology is not the solution to the problem of moralism. Swinging the pendulum too far in the other direction has never effectively combated error. True, for a time, people may feel refreshed, but eventually the initial boost of the "Pepsi" begins to cause damage if that is the sum total of the preaching diet they are under! Sanctification is not "simply" the art of getting used to our justification, however appealing that dictum may sound.

9. Tullian Tchividjian, *Jesus + Nothing = Everything* (Wheaton, IL: Crossway, 2011), 95.

10. Ibid., 96. For a better analysis of how to understand "fear and trembling," see Francis Turretin, *Institutes of Elenctic Theology*, ed. James T. Dennison Jr., trans. George Musgrave Giger (Phillipsburg, NJ: P&R Publishing, 1992), 15.17.29.

11. Tchividjian, *Jesus + Nothing = Everything*, 49.

Antinomianism comes in various forms. Some preachers preach verse-by-verse, but explain away the true meaning of the passage by the use of "their principles." Others, however, simply do not preach the whole counsel of God. According to Burgess, "That is a perpetual fault among the Anti-nomians, they only pitch upon those places, where Christ and his grace is spoken of; but not of those Texts, where duties are commanded, especially those places of Scripture where the law of God is wonderfully commended, for the many real benefits that come by it."[12] Remaining faithful to the text, not explaining it away or failing to bring home its true import, is easier said than done. Certain hermeneutical principles will cripple even the most gifted preacher. Frequently, antinomians are in more serious error in what they fail to say than in what they do say.

Burgess also highlights the tendency among the antinomians of his day to speak as though they had hegemony over truth, as if they possessed a "new light" or a "higher way" of understanding and speaking God's truth. He writes: "Do not affect applause among people, as having found some new higher way about Christ and grace, than others have. I have observed this itching humour in the Antinomian Sermons printed; where they will call upon their hearers to mark, it may be they shall hear that, which they have not heard before, when the thing is either false; or, if it be true, is no more than ordinarily taught by others."[13] The rhetoric one often hears today has to do with "getting it." That someone "gets grace" often really means that "it does not matter what we do." Condescending talk abounds from the lips of modern-day antinomians who think they alone have understood what grace is.

Burgess is not finished, however. In the last place, he argues that the antinomian actually overthrows grace and Christ in practice: "For he sets up the free grace and Christ, not who names it often in his Book, or in the Pulpit, but whose heart is inwardly and deeply affected with it. Now, who will most heartily and experimentally set up Christ and grace of those two, who urges no use of the law, who takes away the sense or bitterness of sin, who denies humiliation; or he who discovers his defects by the perfect rule of the law, whose soul is . . . humbled because of these defects? Certainly, this latter will much more in heart,

12. Burgess. *Vindiciae legis*, 270.
13. Ibid.

117

and real affections set up free grace."[14] Many preachers lack penetrating application and conviction. But conviction of heart and a profound sense of sin are actually signs of the Spirit's presence in preaching (Acts 2:37).

Similarly, Rutherford seems hardly impressed that there "be volumes written of Christ, Sermon upon Sermon, and not line upon line only, but book upon book, and Tome upon Tome."[15] He adds, "In this learned Age, when Antinomians write book after book of Christ, I should say, for all their crying, O the Gospel-spirit, the Gospel-strain of Preaching, the Mystery of free grace . . . that one ounce, one grain of the spiritual and practical knowledge of Christ is more to be valued than talent-weights, yea, ship-loads, or mountains of knowledge of the dumb school-letter."[16] It is not enough simply to mention grace or even Christ often in a sermon. Some of the most boring sermons mention them frequently. And that is precisely one of the dangers of antinomian preaching: it becomes boring. The same repetitive mantras are preached week after week, to the point that if you have heard one sermon, you have heard them all. These are not overstatements. It is very difficult for some preachers to deliver messages each week when they have a sort of "systematic theology" that they need to declare every Lord's Day. Sonship advocates, for example, are often guilty of this very thing. Despite the popularity of such adjectives as "scandalous" and "radical," many preachers who use these terms to describe grace and the gospel are not quite as shocking as they believe themselves to be. Indeed, good Christology should never be boring, but the richness of Reformed Christology has been lost in favor of clichés. Christ should be in every sermon, as we see in apostolic example and teaching. Preaching the whole Christ prevents us from becoming monotonous in our so-called gospel summaries at the end of every sermon.

DIFFERENT GENRES

Apart from Richard Coore, those who have been described as seventeenth-century antinomians did not view themselves as antinomians. Few today would wish to be described as antinomian. The difficulty for

14. Ibid., 271.
15. Samuel Rutherford, *Christ dying and drawing sinners to himself* (London, 1647), "To the Reader."
16. Ibid.

anyone wishing to make use of the term to describe someone's theology has always been keenly felt. Even in the seventeenth century, the analysis of antinomianism changes because the texts change. Early seventeenth-century antinomian writings are typically ultra-polemical. Sometimes they are incomplete sermon notes, not works of systematic theology. Moreover, the caliber of theological minds in the seventeenth century was wide ranging. Men like John Bunyan (bap. 1628, d. 1688) and Edward Fisher were not trained theologians in the same mold as, say, John Davenant and John Owen. Therefore, one notes obvious differences in their writing styles and their manner of expressing theology. Owen's precision was rarely matched by his contemporaries, and the antinomians simply could not match Owen for clarity, as was crucial in the context of such vigorous debate.

Sermons are not expected to be as sophisticated as theological treatises. There is a place for hyperbole in our theological discourse, particularly in our sermonizing. Our congregations need to be shocked sometimes with statements that "wake them up." All too often, Reformed sermons have more in common with Owen's systematic manner of speaking than they do with the examples of preaching in Scripture. For example, Jesus frequently said things that were incongruous and bizarre. David Seccombe, in his excellent analysis of this principle in Jesus' teaching, shows how he used parabolic one-liners and images to get across his points that, on close examination, reveal incongruity, exaggeration, and the bizarre.[17] The parables, especially the parable of the mustard seed (Mark 4:30–32), are simply ludicrous if we stop and think about them for one moment. But Christ also speaks of eating his flesh (John 6:53–56), cutting off body parts (Mark 9:43–47), and the camel trying to go through the eye of a needle (Mark 10:25). As Seccombe notes, "There are others too which catch the attention, sometimes by exaggeration, sometimes by their violence, and sometimes by their incongruity—at least they would have once; the modern reader is desensitised by familiarity and the tendency to read 'religiously.'"[18] Like Jesus, the prophet Ezekiel, said (often) and did (Ezek. 4:12) things that likely would not get him invited to some of the popular evangelical and Reformed conferences!

Perhaps from time to time preachers must say things that wake their listeners up to the reality of their sin and the reality of God's grace by saying

17. David Seccombe, "Incongruity in the Gospel Parables," *Tyndale Bulletin* 62, 2 (2011): 161–72.
18. Ibid., 164. Seccombe cites Mark 3:35; 7:27; 8:33, 34; 9:35; 11:23; 14:24.

things that shock the modern hearer. Regarding the former, it was Luther who once said to his wife Katie that he was like a loose stool and the world was like a big anus, and they were about to depart from one another.[19] In this example, Luther brings home the reality of what we are as sinners and what this world is in its sin and misery (i.e., its bondage to corruption, Rom. 8:21). The rhetoric in that instance should keep us from loving this world as much as we do. On the other hand, the beauty of God's grace in the person of his Son, whereby sinners are justified freely apart from works, will inevitably cause people to stumble. The Christian message is antithetical to every other religious system. For this reason, sometimes the message of justification by faith alone will be misunderstood and/or leave people utterly dumbfounded that God should accept them "by pardoning their sins, and by accounting and accepting their persons as righteous; not for any thing wrought in them, or done by them, but for Christ's sake alone; not by imputing faith itself, the act of believing, or any other evangelical obedience to them, as their righteousness; but by imputing the obedience and satisfaction of Christ unto them, they receiving and resting on him and his righteousness by faith; which faith they have not of themselves, it is the gift of God" (WCF 11.1). Perhaps people will misunderstand this doctrine and accuse the preacher of antinomianism.

The apostle Paul may have been subject to the same type of critique, though we should be careful not to be anachronistic here. Whatever claims were being made against the apostle's teaching, even by Jewish Christians who were uncomfortable with his gospel, the problem of antinomianism as defined in this book should not be equated with the charge that was likely made against his teaching. The moralism of our contemporary church was not quite the same thing as the "Torah-ism" of first-century Christians. Christians should not keep on sinning that grace may abound (Rom. 6:1) because they have died to sin. Some argue that Paul answers the "antinomian" charge with gospel, not with law, in Romans 6:2ff.[20] That point is true, but it needs to be added that Paul responds specifically with the reality of our definitive sanctification (v. 2), as well as Christ's definitive

19. See Martin Luther's "Tabletalk" in *Luther's Works*, ed. Jaroslav Pelikan and Helmut T. Lehmann, American Edition (Philadelphia: Muehlenberg and Fortress, and St. Louis: Concordia, 1955–86), 54:448.
20. Note also that he does not embrace the charge of "lawlessness," as if the charge were a badge of honor!

sanctification (v. 10), and then presses home the reality that we are obedient slaves of God (progressive sanctification).[21] A similar scenario emerges in Romans 6:15–16, "What then? Are we to sin because we are not under law but under grace? By no means! Do you not know that if you present yourselves to anyone as obedient slaves, you are slaves of the one whom you obey, either of sin, which leads to death, or of obedience, which leads to righteousness?" The response to the problem of whether God's grace will lead God's people to licentiousness is emphatically denied by Paul's teaching of definitive and progressive sanctification. Paul could hardly be accused of antinomianism in his writing and preaching, based on what we read in Romans 6 (see also 1 Cor. 7:19).[22]

What is in fact important is not whether preachers say things from time to time, as they make use of rhetorical devices like hyperbole, that sound "antinomian" or "legalistic," but whether, during a sustained course of ministry, they give the impression that they preach Christ and preach the imperatives that God, in his wisdom, thinks his people need to hear. It is hardly fair to anyone to take one sermon and criticize a preacher for not focusing enough on this or that, but when the preacher consistently fails to exhort his people or consistently fails to preach sermons that display the glories of Christ, there is a problem. The antinomians failed, not only in the former, but also in the latter. In fact, antinomian preachers, for all their insistence on the gospel, actually preached a half-gospel that mitigates the transformative aspects of union with Christ. They treated Christians as still totally depraved, not much different from when they were in their state of wrath. But transformation must necessarily take place in the Christian life in terms of law keeping because Christians are being conformed to the image of Christ (Rom. 8:29).

21. On definitive sanctification, see John Murray, *Collected Writings of John Murray* (Edinburgh: Banner of Truth, 1976–82), 2:277–93.

22. There are other places in the Scriptures where Paul is accused of turning people away from Moses (Acts 21:21). His response to the charge of "antinomianism" in the following verses is interesting (vv. 22–26).

9

TOWARD A DEFINITION AND A SOLUTION

"CHRISTIAN READER, IF THIS TREATISE MAY SEEM TO ANY TO BE SUPERFLUOUS, AS DEFENDING THAT, WHICH NO GOOD CHRISTIANS DENY: YET CONSIDERING HOW FRUITFUL THESE LAST TIMES ARE IN BRINGING FORTH THE SPURIOUS SPAWNS, AND MONSTROUS BIRTHS OF ALL KINDS OF HERESIES, AMONG WHICH THIS OF THE ANTINOMIANS."
—HENRY BURTON[1]

THEOLOGY IS NOT EASY, particularly because of the indwelling sin that remains in us. Theology is even more difficult when polemics are involved. There can be little doubt that defining antinomianism is exceedingly difficult, to the point that even discussing a number of shared characteristics is not without its problems. In my view, a book on legalism would also encounter the same types of problems. Many understand "legalism" as salvation by works, which is only partly true. This way of understanding the concept ends up missing the more subtle forms of legalistic thinking that creep into our thinking. If antinomianism is understood simply as all indicatives without imperatives, and legalism simply as all imperatives

1. Henry Burton, *The law and the gospell reconciled* (London, 1631), "To the Reader."

without indicatives, then there have been very few true antinomians or true legalists in the Christian tradition. Legalistic thinking suffers from the same types of subtle errors as antinomianism. Indeed, they share the same fundamental problem: poor Christology. In this book, a number of areas have been identified where seventeenth-century antinomian theologians differed from their orthodox Reformed counterparts. While examining the nature, context, and issues involved in antinomianism, I have endeavored to show that the true solution to antinomianism must have in view the person and work of Christ, properly understood.

Antinomianism must not be confused with the etymological meaning of *antinomian* (i.e., "against the law"). There is some overlap, of course, but the historical debates focused on more specific areas of the Christian life. Thus, in attempting to arrive at a definition of antinomianism, we have not understood the debate if we simply identify antinomians as those who flatly reject the use and necessity of the moral law in the life of the Christian.

ANTINOMIAN CHARACTERISTICS

This book has focused on a certain type of antinomianism that has been characterized by historians as the "imputative" strain that emerged in England during the seventeenth century.[2] Of course, orthodox Reformed theologians affirmed the imputation of Christ's righteousness to believers who receive and rest upon him alone as he is offered in the gospel. But the imputative antinomians extrapolated many unsound views from the doctrine of justification. Indeed, Sinclair Ferguson's response to the Lutheran theologian Gerhard Forde could very well describe the Reformed response to antinomian theology in the seventeenth century. Ferguson notes that Forde gives such a priority to the doctrine of justification "that it not only dominates sanctification, but at times even seems to threaten to displace the person of Christ from center stage."[3] Ferguson adds that when union with

---

2. There are other matters that could have been discussed. For example, there was a peculiar relationship between antinomianism and spiritualism. Particularly in the New England controversy, the line between the saved and the unsaved depended on the inward possession of the Holy Spirit. The antinomians (according to Johannes Hoornbeeck) adopted a universalistic view of the Atonement. So to avoid universalism, people looked for evidence of the work of the Holy Spirit in order to identify those who were saved. Therefore, antinomianism became, in the end, very introspective.

3. Donald Alexander, ed., *Christian Spirituality: Five Views of Sanctification* (Downers Grove, IL: InterVarsity Press, 1988), 34.

Christ "is made the architectonic principle of the application of redemption . . . the tension which Lutheranism seems to feel *between* justification and the Christian's good work, or sanctification, begins to vanish."[4] While recognizing that there are different emphases and positions within Lutheran theology, there can be little doubt that it has some antinomian tendencies, particularly as espoused by Forde. But what, in sum, did seventeenth-century antinomian theology look like in contrast to orthodox Reformed theology?

In the first place, in orthodox Christianity, imitating Christ as our pattern of holiness is essential to the Christian life. In the context of the Christian life, the Spirit so works in believers that they have not been deprived of their wills, but rather in such a way that our obedience is truly our obedience. The faith that is a gift of God is nevertheless our faith. The power comes from God; the act belongs to man. But the antinomians tended not only to ridicule the idea that we must attempt to conform our lives to the pattern of Christ, but also to suggest that any work we perform is not our work but Christ's.

The antinomians also rejected the idea that the law, accompanied by the Spirit, is a true means of sanctification. Just as the preaching of the gospel, apart from the accompanying power of the Spirit, cannot sanctify, so too is the law unable to sanctify without the Spirit. Conversely, however, both the gospel and the law are able to sanctify as long as they are accompanied by the Holy Spirit. That is to say, the means used by God to sanctify—the peculiar work of the Spirit—includes the moral law of God. Connected to this idea is the view that Christians must obey the law of God because it is the law of Christ, who is our lawgiver. We do not obey only if we are willing to do so, but even if we are not entirely willing. But the antinomians recoiled from the idea that Christians do what is good and refrain from what is evil because God's law says so. They also failed to appreciate that the commanding power of the law is actually heightened in the new covenant because the indicatives in the new covenant are heightened. The demands of the law are intensified because Christians are living now in the age of the Spirit, in which the promises of God have been fulfilled in the death, resurrection, ascension, enthronement, and intercession of Christ.

A further area of dispute between the antinomians and Reformed theologians had to do with the relationship between the law and the gospel. No

4. Ibid.

125

Reformed writer disputed that the law and the gospel were utterly opposed to one another when it came to the doctrine of justification. The precise point of contention centered on the law-gospel distinction in the Christian life. For the Christian, the law is his friend because God and Christ are his friends—that is, the law and the gospel "sweetly comply." The notion of a radical opposition between the law and the gospel, whereby the law only commands and the gospel only promises, has more in common with antinomian theology than Reformed theology. In fact, such Reformed theologians as John Owen spoke about the "prescriptive part of the gospel." When a sharp distinction is maintained between the law and the gospel in the Christian life, the first use of the law tends to replace the third use of the law as its primary function.[5] Despite claims to the contrary, the law takes on a decidedly negative tone in the preaching and writing of those who hold to such a sharp distinction. For Reformed theologians who speak of a promising and commanding gospel, the graciousness of the gospel is shown by the fact that God accepts our sincere, albeit imperfect, obedience. He could not do that if we sought to be justified by the law. For this reason, the Christian life is not one of despair because we cannot obey our Father—far from it. Our Father, in his grace toward us in Christ, accepts our obedience and may even refer to his people as righteous and blameless, despite their imperfect obedience (Luke 1:6).

The goodness of God toward his people is evident in the way in which he rewards our good works. In opposition to the antinomians, Reformed theologians spoke of our works as necessary for salvation and as genuinely good. These good works, done according to God's law, by faith and in the power of the Spirit, are rewarded. Bullinger, Pictet, Wollebius, Davenant, Turretin, and the Westminster divines, to name but a few, all insisted that good works are necessary for salvation. But they also affirmed that these works are from God, lead to God, and are rewarded by God for the sake of his Son, Jesus Christ. There is not the slightest hint of moralism or legalism in Reformed treatments of good works. But antinomian preachers do not emphasize rewards for good works, and thus deprive Christians of the knowledge of God's grace.

5. Note Ferguson's response to Forde: "Lutheranism has had a deep reluctance to highlight the so-called 'third-use of the law' (as a rule for life)." Ibid., 35. The absolute law-gospel antithesis probably accounts for this problem in a certain strain of Lutheran thinking.

Not surprisingly, the antinomians loved to echo the phrase that God does not love us any more or any less on the basis of our obedience or lack thereof. But that is not the whole story. Reformed divines spoke of a two-fold love of God for his creatures. His benevolent love, which is primary, is eternal, unchangeable, and unconditional. There is nothing we can do or not do to merit this love. However, God and Christ have a love of complacency for their people, which has in view the communion that takes place between them and their people (John 14:21, 23). This complacent love is not static, but can increase or decrease based on our obedience or disobedience. For this reason, God and Christ really are pleased and displeased with Christians. The antinomians, with their view that God sees no sin in his people, asserted that God could not be angry with his people. But it is not pastorally helpful to tell Christians that God cannot get angry with them when in fact he can and does (Pss. 38–39). Repentance and forgiveness are aspects of the Christian life that should occur daily (Matt. 6:12).

The antinomian theologians had various views, but their ideas on assurance held them all together. In their yearning to give assurance of salvation to their people, they stripped away a number of biblical truths and attempted to give justification by faith an all-controlling place in the life of the Christian, so that faith in God's promises was supposed to provide assurance to Christians. Reformed theologians in the Puritan era, just as ever since, understood God's promises to be the primary ground for assurance of salvation. But because the gospel is not simply coextensive with justification, but also includes God's promise of renovation (*regeneratio*), they said that it is not only legitimate but necessary to look also to Christ's work in his people as a ground for assurance. The objective ground is primary, but the subjective flows out of it. The two are not enemies, but friends. What is more, the means that God uses to assure his people are many and varied. There is richness to the Christian life that is undermined by antinomian theologians because of their exclusive focus on one truth at the expense of others.

All of this indicates that one error gives rise to another. Such is the case in Arminianism, in which erroneous doctrines of God, his decrees, and the Atonement lead to a deficient doctrine of justification. Similarly, the antinomians, in making one crucial mistake, such as blurring the impetration and application of redemption, involved themselves in several others.

When all or at least most of these errors are combined in a preaching ministry, you have antinomianism. And, despite loud protestations to the contrary, antinomian theology leads to practical antinomianism, which is a serious problem in the church today.

There is no short and easy way to define antinomianism, unless one regards the phenomenon as a rejection of the third use of the law. But that definition tends to miss the more subtle ways in which antinomians expressed themselves in the past and still do today. From what I have been able to read and hear from Tullian Tchividjian, whether in his books, blogs, conferences, or sermons, he would find himself far more comfortable among the likes of Eaton, Traske, Crisp, and Towne than among the Westminster divines![6] But he is only one example of many; there are others today who have serious leanings in the direction of the seventeenth-century antinomians.

Identifying an antinomian is not easy. Our sins of omission are less obvious, and thus harder to identify, than our sins of commission. This is particularly the case for antinomians. They have a habit of saying mutually contradictory things, as well as affirming truths that they deny in practice. That is, their public ministry is not always in accord with what they will tell you when they are, in private, pressed on certain points. Nonetheless, the charge of antinomianism should only be made carefully, and for that reason I have refrained from implicating certain individuals who have leanings in that direction. I hope that this book will alert them to the errors and dangers of antinomian theology. Yet this book has also tried to put forth a positive solution to the problem of antinomianism by focusing on Reformed Christology.

THE SOLUTION

The solution to antinomianism must be to understand and love the person and work of Christ. Pastors in broadly Reformed circles seem to have a fairly good understanding of the doctrine of justification and the other applied benefits of redemption. But, in my experience, there is a serious lack of understanding of Christ's person, sometimes to the point that ordained ministers entertain heretical ideas about it (e.g., that Christ has only one will). Christ's truly human experiences, including his faith, hope,

6. He would also have more in common with the Lutheran writer Gerhard Forde than with the Reformed writer Sinclair Ferguson.

and love, as well as the promises by which he lived, provide the pattern for his own people because of our union with him. Our union with him in his death and resurrection guarantees that the blessings we receive from God all come through and in our Savior. But this reality also guarantees the shape and nature of the Christian life insofar as we live our lives in a manner similar to Christ's. He obeyed, prayed, learned, and trusted. Our union with him requires that we likewise obey, pray, learn, and trust. He received his reward, and we likewise will receive our reward. He depended upon the work of the Spirit for his obedience, even his obedience to death on the cross (Heb. 9:14). We must likewise depend entirely on the Holy Spirit for our obedience, as we live by faith (as Christ did). If Christ understood that his obedience pleased his Father, as well as that disobedience would have displeased him, then Christians must likewise acknowledge that the same is true for them. The stakes were infinitely higher for Christ—our salvation depended on his perfect obedience—but the principle remains true for his people.

Christ is not only the pattern for our Christian life, but also the source of our Christian life. We are able to obey the law and please God, not because of something intrinsic in us, but because of Christ's resurrection power at work in us. The triune God lives in his people. The Father (1 John 4:12–13), the Spirit (Rom. 8:11), and Christ (Eph. 3:17) all take up residence in the elect.[7] The resurrected Christ dwells in his people, empowering them, assuring and comforting them, convicting them, and transforming them. The realities of the new covenant should never cause us to live with an under-realized eschatology, whereby Christians are assumed to be not much different—apart from a sentence that has been passed on them—than an unbeliever.[8] But neither should we slip into the error of perfectionism, or an over-realized eschatology. Nonetheless,

7. On Christ dwelling in our hearts, see Thomas Goodwin, "A Sermon on Ephesians III.17," in *The Works of Thomas Goodwin, D.D.* (1861–66; repr., Grand Rapids: Reformation Heritage Books, 2006), 2:391–406. This is one of the finest sermons I have ever read.

8. John Owen makes a number of salient comments on the nature of indwelling sin in the believer that clarify the typical Reformed position on this question. He argues that there is, through grace, "kept up in believers a constant and ordinarily prevailing will of doing good, notwithstanding the power and efficacy of indwelling sin to the contrary." So believers, even in their worst condition, are distinguished from unbelievers in their best condition! Owen adds, "In believers there is a will of doing good, an habitual disposition and inclination in their wills unto that which is spiritually good." He is not unaware of the power of indwelling sin in believers, but at the same time he points out that there is a decided difference between sin in an unbeliever and sin in a believer. *The Works*

the horrible reality of indwelling sin should continually remind us of our need and duty to mortify sin by the Spirit (Rom. 8:13), who comes in the name of Christ to believers (Rom. 8:9). To the degree that good Reformed Christology informs the preaching and teaching ministries of pastors and theologians, we will have all of the necessary tools to fight what Rutherford called "the Golden white devil"[9] by means of the one who is "chief among ten thousand" (Song 5:10).

---

of John Owen, D.D., ed. William H. Goold (Edinburgh: Johnstone & Hunter, 1850–55), 6:159–60. On the power of indwelling sin, I am in basic agreement with Owen's view in volume 6 of his *Works*.

9. Samuel Rutherford's description of antinomianism in *A sermon preached to the Honorable House of Commons: at their late solemne fast, Wednesday, Janu. 31. 1643* (London, 1644), 32.

BIBLIOGRAPHY

PRIMARY SOURCES

Acta of Handelingen der Nationale Synode, in den naam onzes Heeren Jezus Christus, gehouden door autoriteit der Hoogmogende Heeren Staten-Generaal der Vereenigde Nederlanden te Dordrecht, ten jare 1618 en 1619. Edited by J. H. Donner and S. A. van den Hoorn. Leiden: D. Donner, 1883–86.

Acta Synodi Nationalis, in nomine Domini nostri Jesu Christi. Dordrechti: Isaaci Joannidis Canini, 1620.

Ames, William. *The Marrow of Theology.* Grand Rapids: Baker Books, 1997.

———. *A Sketch of the Christian's Catechism.* Translated by Todd M. Rester. Grand Rapids: Reformation Heritage Books, 2008.

Augustine, *Confessions.* Translated by R. S. Pine-Coffin. London: Penguin Books, 1961.

———. "Grace and Free Choice." In *Answer to the Pelagians, IV: To the Monks of Hadrumetum and Provence,* translated by Roland J. Teske. New York: New City Press, 1999.

Baxter, Richard. *A Treatise of Justifying Righteousness in Two Books.* London: Nevil Simons & Jonathan Robinson, 1676.

Bedford, Thomas. *An Examination of the Chief Points of Antinomianism.* London, 1646.

Blake, Thomas. *Vindiciæ Foederis.* London, 1658.

Bullinger, Heinrich. *In sanctissimam Pauli ad Romanos Epistolam.* Zurich, 1533.

Burgess, Anthony. *The True Doctrine of Justification Asserted and Vindicated, from the Errours of Papists, Arminians, Socinians, and more especially Antinomians.* 2nd ed. London: Tho. Underhill, 1651.

———. *Vindiciae legis: or, A vindication of the morall law and the covenants, from the Errours of Papists, Arminians, Socinians, and more especially Antinomians.* London: T. Underhill, 1646.

Burton, Henry. *The law and the gospell reconciled*. London, 1631.

Calvin, John. *Institutes of the Christian Religion*. Edited by John T. McNeill. Translated by Ford Lewis Battles. 2 vols. Philadelphia: Westminster Press, 1960.

Charnock, Stephen. *The Works of Stephen Charnock*. 5 vols. Edinburgh: James Nichol, 1865.

Chauncy, Isaac. *Neonomianism unmask'd; or, The ancient gospel pleaded against the other, called a new law or gospel in a theological debate, occasioned by a book lately wrote by Mr. Dan. Williams*. London, 1692.

Crisp, Tobias. *Christ alone exalted, being the compleat works of Tobias Crisp, D.D., containing XLII sermons*. London, 1690.

Davenant, John. *A Treatise on Justification*. Translated by Josiah Allport. London, 1844.

Denne, Henry. *Grace, mercy, and peace*. London, 1645.

Duncan, John. *Colloquia Peripatetica*. Edinburgh: Edmonston & Douglas, 1873.

Durham, James. *A Commentarie upon the Book of the Revelation*. Amsterdam, 1660.

Eaton, John. *The discovery of the most dangerous dead faith*. London, 1642.

————. *The honey-combe of free justification by Christ alone*. London, 1642.

Edwards, Jonathan. *The Works of Jonathan Edwards*. 2 vols. Peabody, MA: Hendrickson, 2003.

Flavel, John. *The Works of the Rev. Mr. John Flavel*. 1820; repr., Edinburgh: Banner of Truth, 1997.

Gill, John. *A Collection of Sermons and Tracts*. 3 vols. London: George Keith, 1773–78.

Goodwin, Thomas. *The Works of Thomas Goodwin, D.D.* 12 vols. 1861–66; repr., Grand Rapids: Reformation Heritage Books, 2006.

Hopkins, Ezekiel. *The Works of Ezekiel Hopkins*. 4 vols. London: L. B. Seeley, 1809.

Hopkins, Samuel. *The Works of Samuel Hopkins*. 3 vols. Boston: Doctrinal Tract and Book Society, 1854.

Jugement du Synode National des Eglises Reformees du Pays-Bas, tenu à Dordrecht l'An 1618 et 1619. Nismes: Jean Vaguenar, 1620.

Leigh, Edward. *A Treatise of Divinity*. London: William Lee, 1646.

Leydekker, Melchior. *De verborgentheid des geloofs eenmaal den heiligen overgelevert, of het kort begryp der ware godsgeleerdheid beleden in de Gereformeerde Kerk*. Rotterdam, 1700.

Luther, Martin. *Luther's Works*. Edited by Jaroslav Pelikan and Helmut T. Lehmann. American Edition. 55 vols. Philadelphia: Muehlenberg and Fortress, and St. Louis: Concordia, 1955–86.

Maccovius, Johannes. *Scholastic Discourse: Johannes Maccovius (1588–1644) on Theological and Philosophical Distinctions and Rules.* Apeldoorn: Instituut voor Reformatieonderzoek, 2009.

Owen, John. *The Works of John Owen, D.D.* Edited by William H. Goold. 24 vols. Edinburgh: Johnstone & Hunter, 1850–55.

Richardson, Samuel. *Divine consolations.* London, 1649.

Rutherford, Samuel. *Christ dying and drawing sinners to himself.* London, 1647.

————. *A survey of the spirituall antichrist.* 2 parts. London, 1647.

————. *The Tryal & Triumph of Faith.* London, 1645.

Saltmarsh, John. *Free Grace.* London, 1645.

Shepard, Thomas. *The parable of the ten virgins opened & applied, being the substance of divers sermons on Matth. 25, 1–13 wherein the difference between the sincere Christian and the . . . hypocrite . . . are clearly discovered.* London, 1660.

————. *The Works of Thomas Shepard.* 3 vols. Boston: Doctrinal Tract and Book Society, 1853.

Sibbes, Richard. *The Returning Backslider.* London, 1639.

————. *The Works of the Reverend Richard Sibbes.* 3 vols. Aberdeen: J. Chalmers, 1809.

Towne, Robert. *The Assertion of Grace.* London, 1645.

————. *A Re-assertion of Grace . . . A Vindication of the Gospel-truths, from the unjust censure and undue aspersions of Antinomians.* London, 1654.

Turretin, Francis. *Institutes of Elenctic Theology.* Edited by James T. Dennison Jr. Translated by George Musgrave Giger. 3 vols. Phillipsburg, NJ: P&R Publishing, 1992–97.

————. *Recueil de sermons sur divers textes de l'Ecriture S. pour l'état présent de l'Eglise.* Genève: Samuel de Tournes, 1686.

Ursinus, Zacharias. *The Commentary of Dr. Zacharias Ursinus on the Heidelberg Catechism.* Translated by G. W. Williard. Cincinnati: Elm Street Printing Company, 1888.

Van Mastricht, Peter. *Theoretico-practica theologia, qua, per singula capita Theologica, pars exegetica, dogmatica, elenchtica & practica, perpetua successione conjugantur.* New ed. Amsterdam, 1724.

Witsius, Herman. *Conciliatory, or Irenical Animadversions, on the Controversies Agitated in Britain, under the unhappy names of Antinomians and Neonomians.* Translated by Thomas Bell. Glasgow: W. Lang, 1807.

Wollebius, Johannes. *Compendium Theologiæ Christianæ.* Amsterdam, 1655.

SECONDARY SOURCES

Alexander, Donald, ed. *Christian Spirituality: Five Views of Sanctification.* Downers Grove, IL: InterVarsity Press, 1988.

Bavinck, Herman. *Reformed Dogmatics.* Vol. 3, *Sin and Salvation in Christ.* Translated by John Vriend. Grand Rapids: Baker, 2006.

Beeke, Joel R. "The Assurance Debate: Six Key Questions." In *Drawn into Controversie: Reformed Theological Diversity and Debates within Seventeenth-Century British Puritanism*, edited by Michael A. G. Haykin and Mark Jones, 263–83. Göttingen: Vandenhoeck & Ruprecht, 2011.

———. *The Quest for Full Assurance: The Legacy of Calvin and His Successors.* Edinburgh: Banner of Truth, 1999.

Beeke, Joel R., and Mark Jones. *A Puritan Theology: Doctrine for Life.* Grand Rapids: Reformation Heritage Books, 2012.

Boersma, Hans. *A Hot Pepper Corn: Richard Baxter's Doctrine of Justification in Its Seventeenth-Century Context of Controversy.* Vancouver: Regent College Publishing, 2003.

Bozeman, Theodore Dwight. *The Precisianist Strain: Disciplinary Religion and Antinomian Backlash in Puritanism to 1638.* Chapel Hill: University of North Carolina Press, 2004.

Coffey, John, and Paul Chang-Ha Lim, eds. *The Cambridge Companion to Puritanism.* Cambridge: Cambridge University Press, 2008.

Como, David. *Blown by the Spirit: Puritanism and the Emergence of an Antinomian Underground in Pre-Civil-War England.* Stanford: Stanford University Press, 2004.

Dennison, James T., Jr., ed. *Reformed Confessions of the 16th and 17th Centuries.* Vol. 2, *1552–1566.* Grand Rapids: Reformation Heritage Books, 2010.

Dingel, Irene. "The Culture of Conflict in the Controversies Leading to the Formula of Concord (1548–1580)." In *Lutheran Ecclesiastical Culture, 1550–1675*, edited by Robert Kolb. Leiden: Brill, 2008.

Edwards, Mark U. *Luther and the False Brethren.* Stanford: Stanford University Press, 1975.

Felt, Joseph B. *The Ecclesiastical History of New England*. 2 vols. Boston: Congregational Library Association, 1855–62.

Ferguson, Sinclair B. *The Holy Spirit*. Contours in Christian Theology. Downers Grove, IL: InterVarsity Press, 1996.

Foord, Martin. "'A New Embassy': John Calvin's Gospel." In *Aspects of Reforming: Theology and Practice in Sixteenth Century Europe*, edited by Michael Parsons. Milton Keynes, UK: Paternoster, 2013.

Gaffin, Richard B, Jr. *"By Faith, Not by Sight": Paul and the Order of Salvation*. Milton Keynes, UK: Paternoster, 2006.

Hall, David D. *The Antinomian Controversy, 1636–1638: A Documentary History*. Durham, NC: Duke University Press, 1990.

Haykin, Michael A. G., and Mark Jones, eds. *Drawn into Controversie: Reformed Theological Diversity and Debates within Seventeenth-Century British Puritanism*. Göttingen: Vandenhoeck & Ruprecht, 2011.

Hendriksen, William. *New Testament Commentary: Exposition of the Gospel according to John*. Grand Rapids: Baker Book House, 1979.

Horton, Michael S. *Putting Amazing Back into Grace: Embracing the Heart of the Gospel*. Grand Rapids: Baker Books, 2002.

————. "Thomas Goodwin and the Puritan Doctrine of Assurance: Continuity and Discontinuity in the Reformed Tradition, 1600–1680." PhD diss., Wycliffe Hall, Oxford, and Coventry University, 1995.

Kevan, Ernest. *The Grace of Law: A Study in Puritan Theology*. Grand Rapids: Soli Deo Gloria Publications, 2003.

Lachman, David C. *The Marrow Controversy, 1718–1723: An Historical and Theological Analysis*. Rutherford Studies in Historical Theology. Edinburgh: Rutherford House, 1988.

Moore, Jonathan D. *English Hypothetical Universalism: John Preston and the Softening of Reformed Theology*. Grand Rapids: Eerdmans, 2007.

Muller, Richard A. *Calvin and the Reformed Tradition: On the Work of Christ and the Order of Salvation*. Grand Rapids: Baker Academic, 2012.

————. *Dictionary of Latin and Greek Theological Terms: Drawn Principally from Protestant Scholastic Theology*. Grand Rapids: Baker, 2001.

————. "A Note on 'Christocentrism' and the Imprudent Use of Such Terminology." *Westminster Theological Journal* 68 (2006): 253–60.

————. *Post-Reformation Reformed Dogmatics*. 4 vols. Grand Rapids, Baker, 2003.

Murray, John. *Principles of Conduct: Aspects of Biblical Ethics*. Grand Rapids: Eerdmans, 1957.

——. *Collected Writings of John Murray.* 4 vols. Edinburgh: Banner of Truth, 1976–82.

O'Donovan, Oliver. *Resurrection and Moral Order: An Outline for Evangelical Ethics.* Leicester: Apollos, 1996.

Oliphint, K. Scott. *God with Us: Divine Condescension and the Attributes of God.* Wheaton, IL: Crossway, 2012.

Packer, J. I. "Introductory Essay." In *The Death of Death in the Death of Christ*, by John Owen. Edinburgh: Banner of Truth, 1999.

Räisänen, Heikki. *Paul and the Law.* Philadelphia: Fortress, 1986.

Seccombe, David. "Incongruity in the Gospel Parables." *Tyndale Bulletin* 62, 2 (2011): 161–72.

Steinmetz, David C. *Luther in Context.* 2nd ed. Grand Rapids: Baker Academic, 2002.

Stoever, William K. *"A Faire and Easie Way to Heaven": Covenant Theology and Antinomianism in Early Massachusetts.* Middletown, CT: Wesleyan University Press, 1978.

Tchividjian, Tullian. *Jesus + Nothing = Everything.* Wheaton, IL: Crossway, 2011.

Van den Brink, G. A. "Calvin, Witsius (1636–1708) and the English Antinomians." In *The Reception of John Calvin and His Theology in Reformed Orthodoxy*, edited by Andreas J. Beck and William den Boer. Leiden: Brill, 2011.

——. *Herman Witsius en het antinomianisme: Met tekst en vertaling van de Animadversiones Irenicae.* Apledoorn: Instituut voor Reformatieonderzoek, 2008.

——. "Impetration and Application and John Owen's Theology." In *The Ashgate Research Companion to John Owen's Theology*, edited by Kelly M. Kapic and Mark Jones. Farnham, UK: Ashgate Publishing, 2012.

Van Dixhoorn, Chad. *The Minutes and Papers of the Westminster Assembly, 1643–1652.* 5 vols. Oxford: Oxford University Press, 2012.

——. "The Strange Silence of Prolocutor Twisse: Predestination and Politics in the Westminster Assembly's Debate over Justification." *Sixteenth Century Journal* 40 (2009): 395–418.

VanDoodewaard, William. "Introduction." In *The Marrow of Modern Divinity*, by Edward Fisher, 17–32. Fearn, UK: Christian Focus Publications, 2009.

Wengert, Timothy J. *Law and Gospel: Philip Melanchthon's Debate with John Agricola of Eisleben over Poenitentia.* Grand Rapids: Baker Books, 1997.

Winship, Michael P. *Making Heretics: Militant Protestantism and Free Grace in Massachusetts, 1636–1641.* Princeton: Princeton University Press, 2002.

INDEX OF SCRIPTURE

49—77
49:1–7—105
50:4–9—105
50:8—23
58—69
64:6—40, 70

Jeremiah
21:33—55

Ezekiel
4:12—119
20:21—47

Matthew
5:6—40
5:8—41, 71
5:16—68
5:20—40
6:12—127
7:21—66–67
11:30—55, 73
16:27—75
17:5—94
23—2
23:23—2
25:34–36—66–67
27:50—107

Mark
1:9–11—105
1:11—94
3:35—119
4:30–32—119
7:8—2, 40
7:27—119
8:33—119
8:34—119
9:2–8—105
9:24—107
9:35—119
9:41—76

9:43–47—119
10:25—119
11:23—119
12:31—28, 37
14:3–6—70
14:24—119

Luke
1:6—52, 71, 126
2:10—46
2:52—24, 88
9:23—76
19:11–26—75
23:46—105

John
1:16—19, 21
3:16—85
3:34—105
3:36—49
6:53–56—119
10:17—88
10:36—57
12:43—2
13—37
13:1—90
13:23—90
13:34—37
14:21—85–86, 90–91, 95, 127
14:21–23—86
14:23—86, 90–91, 95, 127
15:5—15, 71
15:9—90
15:10—23, 86, 88, 91, 105
16:26–27—85
17—77
17:5—57
17:9—90
17:12—90
19:30—58, 89
21:7—90
21:20—90

INDEX OF SUBJECTS AND NAMES